YOUR WORDS

YOUR WORLD

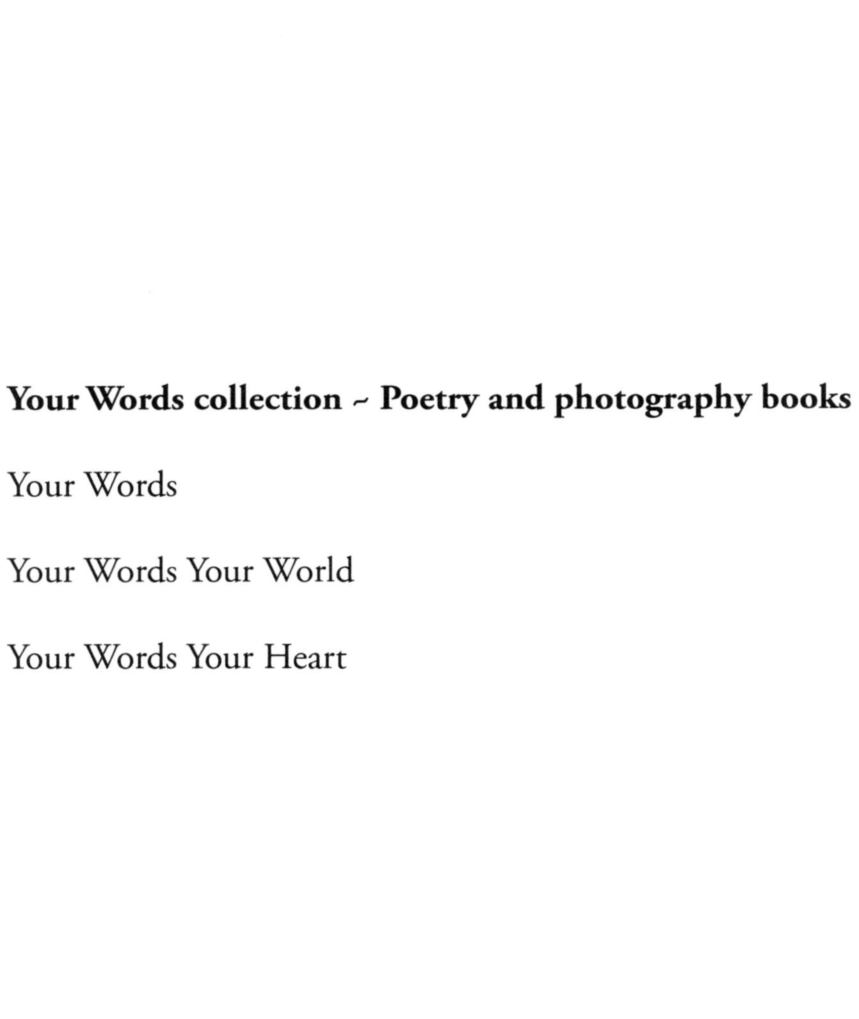

Your Words collection ~ Poetry and photography books

Your Words

Your Words Your World

Your Words Your Heart

Your Words

Your World

Louise Bélanger

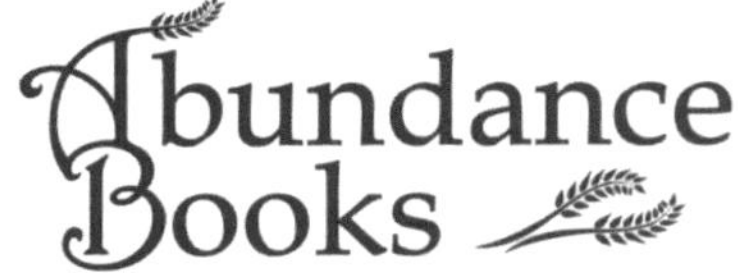

To God

To John, my treasured friend

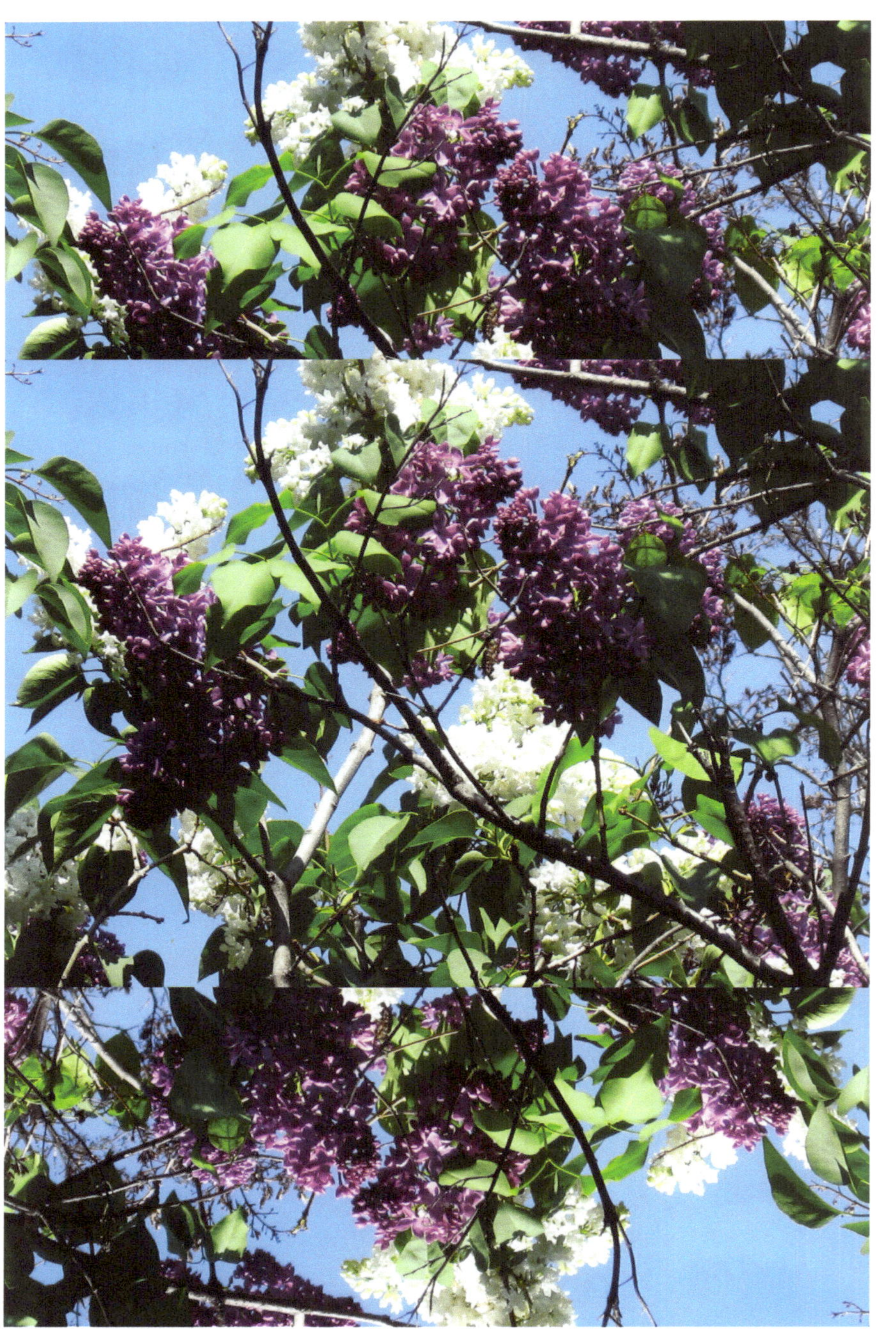

Poems, stories, photographs
All gifts from God

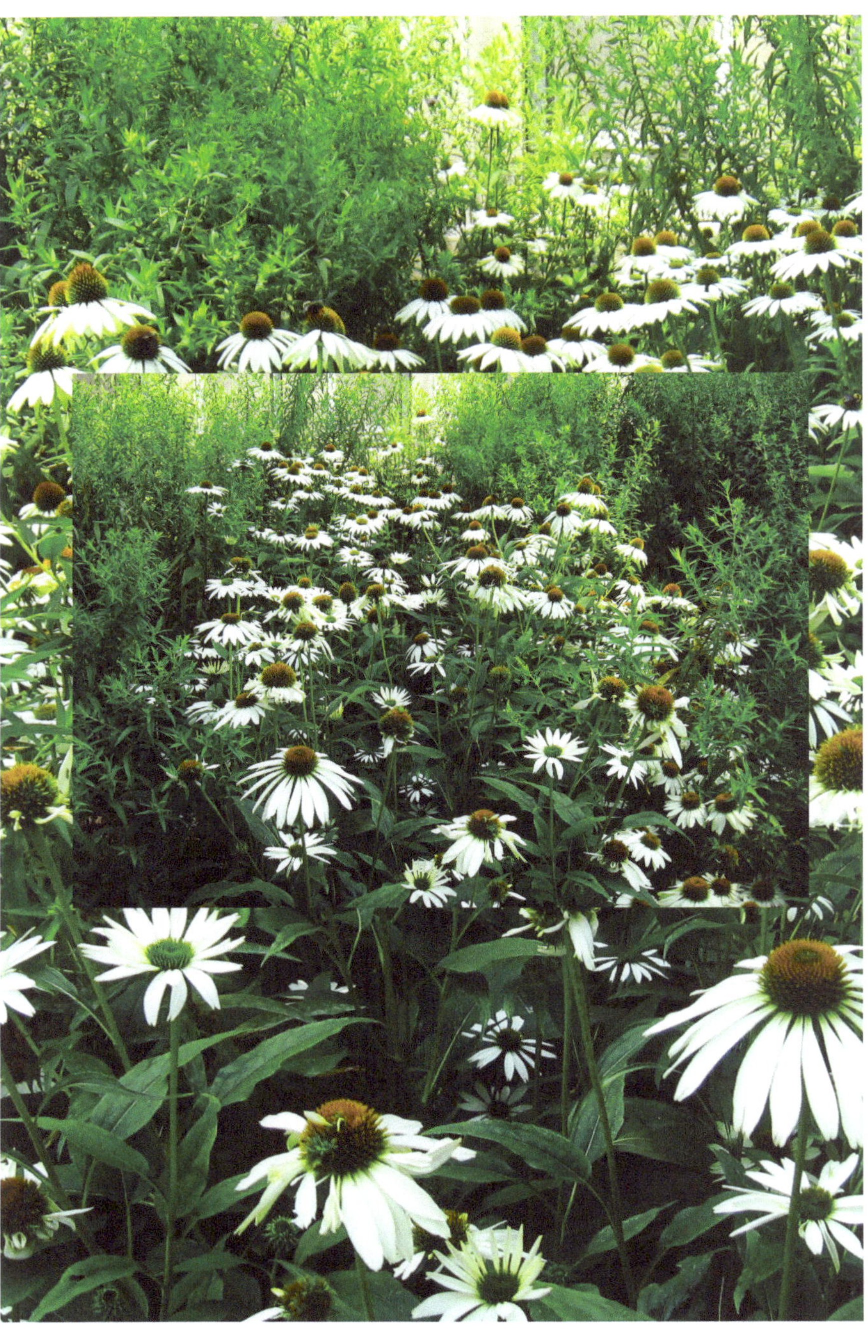

Poems

I want... 13

It is time 16

The contest 19

Ordinary 21

You take the floor away 24

God lifts the veil 27

A handful of cloud 29

Dust 31

During the night 33

"And they lived happily ever after." 36

Gems in Heaven 39

Time and its distant cousin 43

Where God is not there 46

Sometimes... 49

Promises... 53

Did You know? 55

Clowns... 59

Success 61

Don't 65

Rusty and Angel 69

What do you long for? 73

Until you... 76

More than just... 78

A war erupted 85

Now! 88

Zoom to Heaven 92

The most beautiful love poem 94

"Let there be light." 97

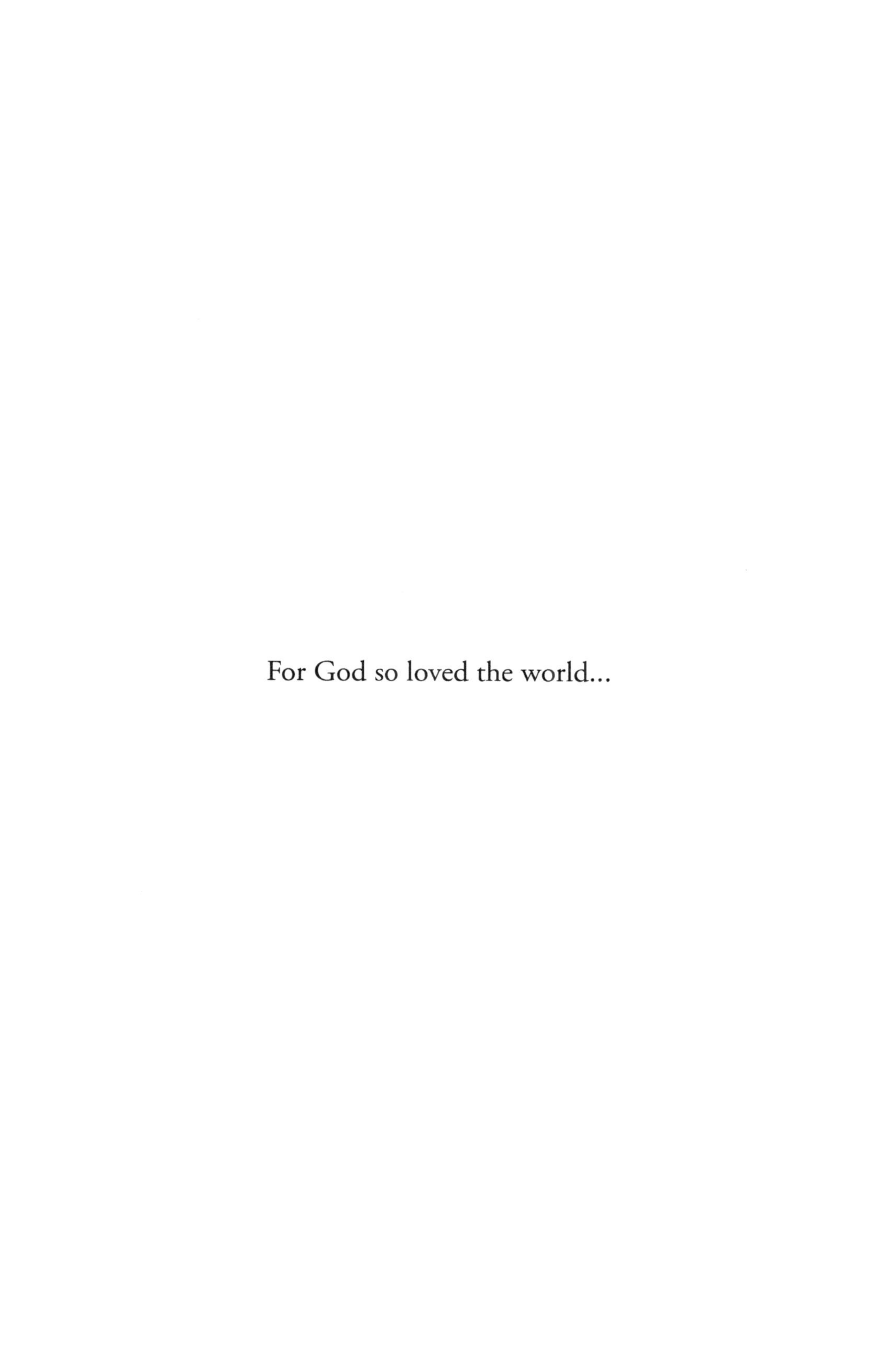

For God so loved the world...

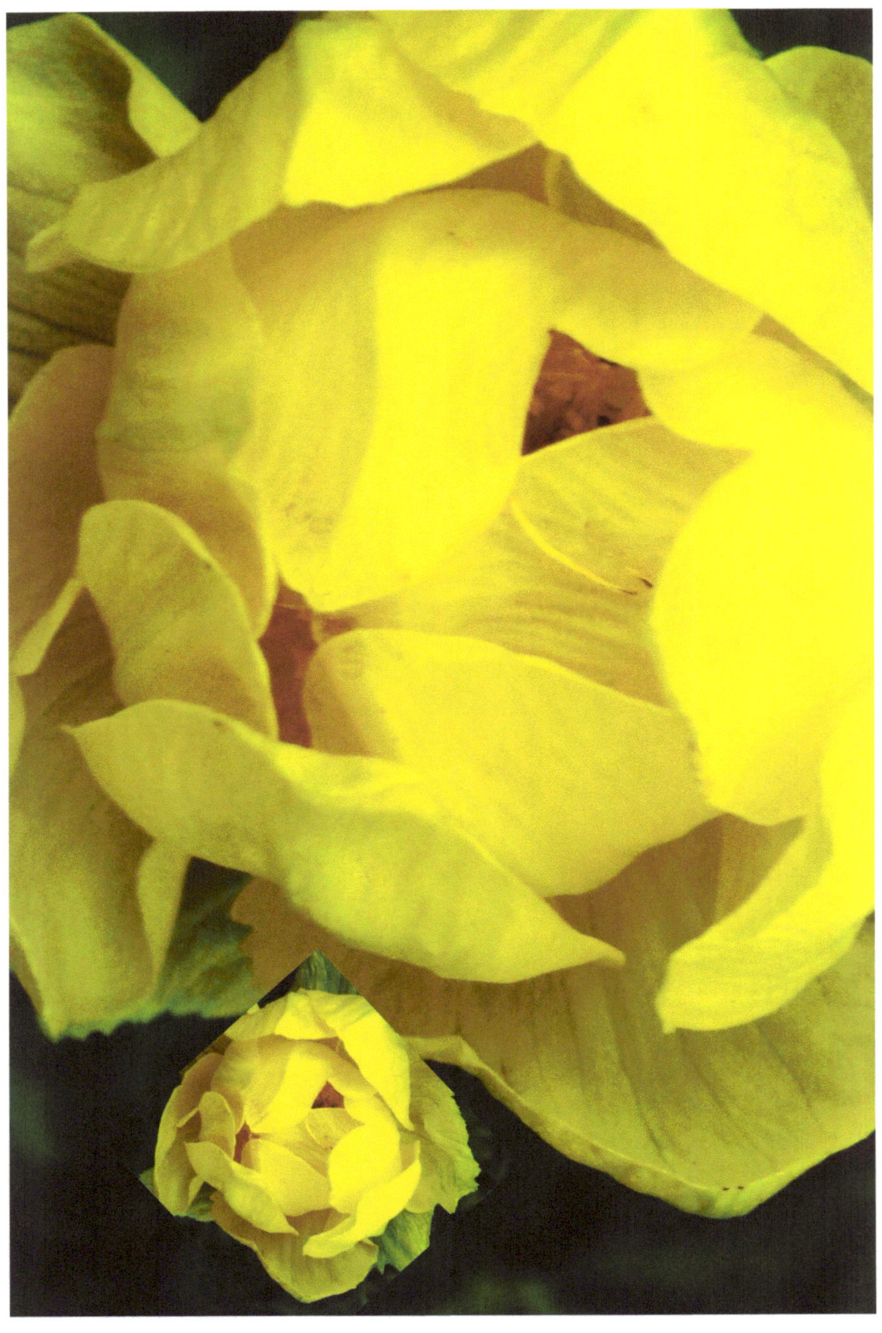

I want...

I want...

Creativity
To explode on the page

Stories and images
Invading my head

To crack open my heart
So it flows on the page

A burst of ideas
Rushing themselves in

I want...

The right word
To describe

What I see, what I feel

What is right, what is wrong
What should be...

God, is there a place?
Where Your Spirit
Takes more room, and I kind of

Disappear

Is there such a place?

Can I choose to go there?

It would be easy then
To fill all these pages

But since...

If there is such a place

I don't know
How to go there

Would You help me instead?
Would You inspire me?

Would You drown me?
In Your talent

Because

I want...

To start writing again

August 15, 2020

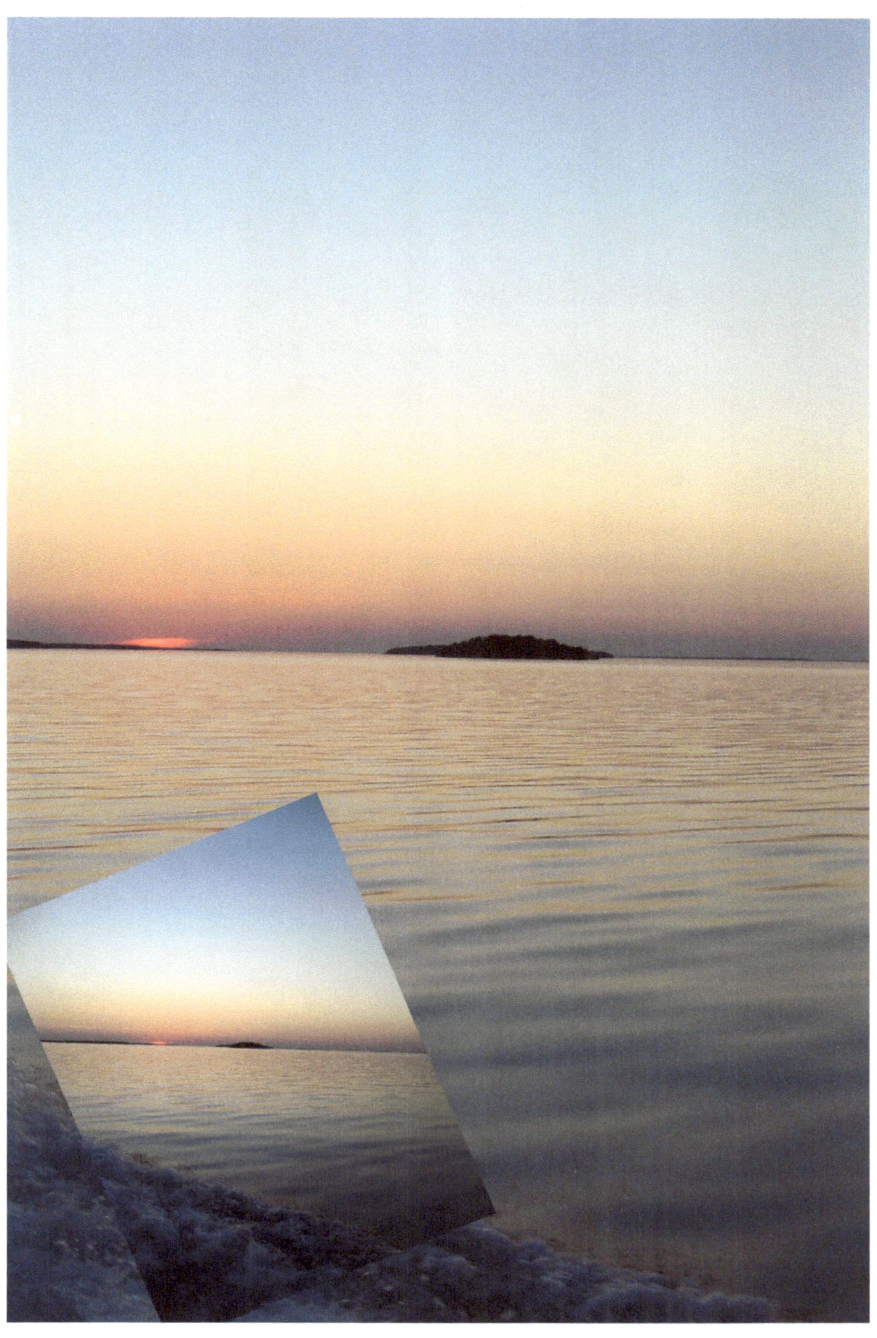

It is time

The man feels the breeze on his cheek
The air is warm enough

It is time

Time to lift the sheets
Sweep the dust, sand the rust

So, he opens the door
And removes all the boards

No more blocking the sun

He brought tools
Some fresh paint and a brush

The new coat makes them look almost real
The chrome is shiny again

He moves the level and the engine roars
The floor starts turning

The music plays
Announcing the up-and-down race

He smiles
His childhood memories flood his mind

He loved to come here when he was a boy
It was his favorite place, all summer long

He remembers seeing his grandfather
Welcoming the crowd

Soon it will be him doing the same

The laughing and the cheering
Will fill the air, once again

Come everyone!

Take a seat on the saddle
Hold the reins, hold them tight

Hear the music
The race is about to start

It is time

Take a ride on Le Carrousel!
The merry-go-round

August 17, 2020

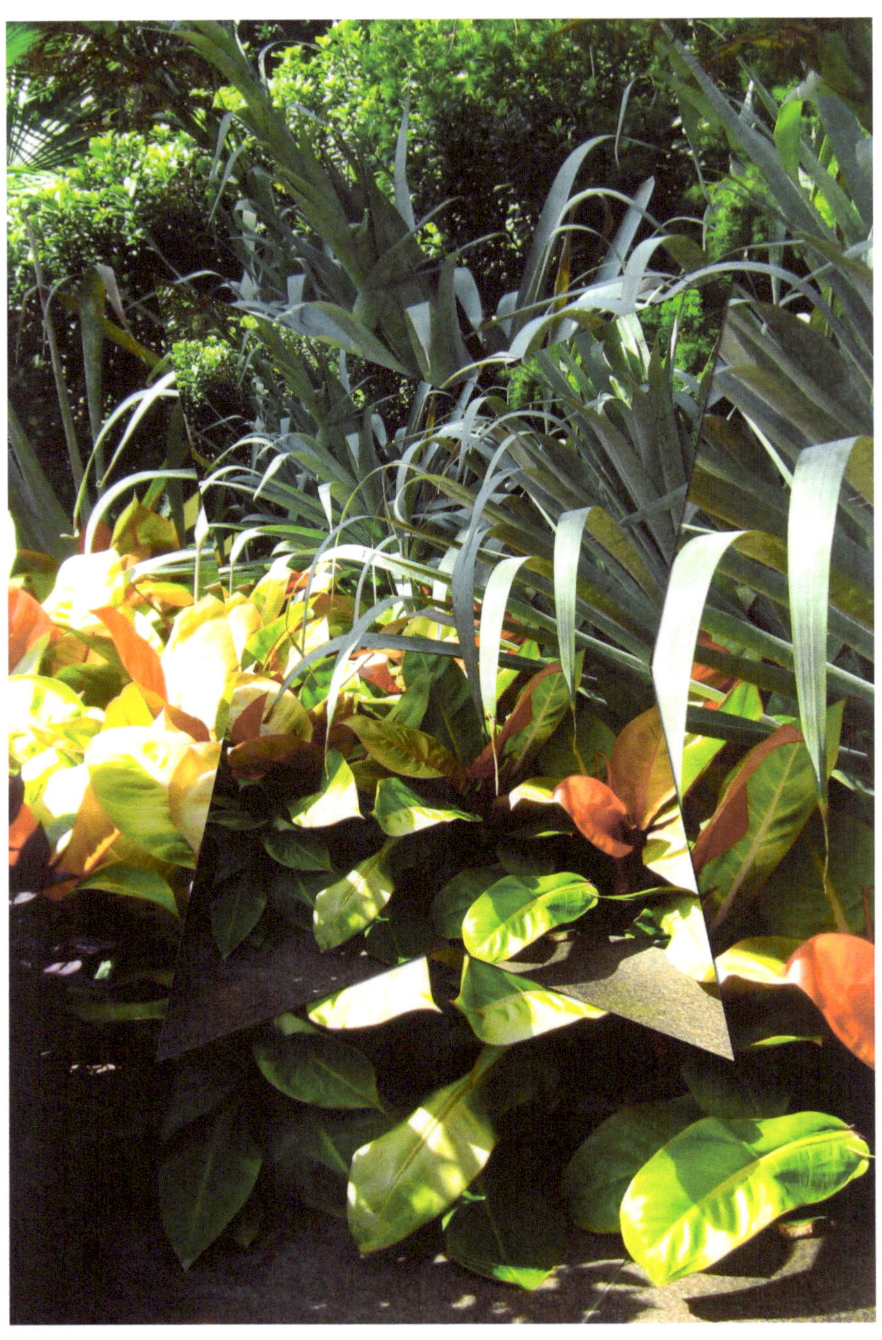

The contest

The flowers had decided
A contest was in order
To declare who was the best

"Well, that's easy," said the rose
"With me, you can express different emotions
I am the best."

"I disagree," said the daisy
"After all, I decide who loves whom
She loves me, she loves me not...he loves me...
Give me the trophy, I won!"

"May I remind you, there is a festival named after me,"
indicated the tulip
"Me too," said the lilac
"I announce spring," shouted the crocus

"I imitate the sun."
"I live on water."
"I grow on trees."

They were all talking over each other until the doorbell rang

They instantly went quiet
A customer had entered the shop

A bouquet was assembled
The purchase was made
The doorbell rang again

At first, the flowers stayed quiet
They did not understand what had occurred
The questions began

"Did you see that?"

"Yes, different flowers were chosen...instead of a few of the same..."

"That made a beautiful bouquet, didn't it?"

"Oh yes! It sure did, it was lovely."

"And the fragrance of each flower
When mixed together was exquisite."

Then they understood
No flower is the best
Separately they don't win the contest
The winning comes when they are together

It is the same with us
God made it so

Each of us has talents
Mine are different than yours
And the same is said for yours

When we work together
Instead of wondering
Who is the best
Each of us uses their talents
For the good of the group

And together...
We are better

And together...
We win

August 19, 2020

Ordinary

A star
In the sky
Is not unique
There are millions of them

But when Jesus was born
A single star
Stopped being
Ordinary

Because of God
It guided the wise men

The Red Sea
If you ask me
Is quite
Ordinary
Just a large pool of water

But when God showed up and parted it
It was
Ordinary
No more

Cloud and fire
God made moving pillars out of them
One by day
One by night
To guide His children
Through the wilderness

Because of God
Ordinary
Disappeared

His power made it so

Many people in the Bible
Considered themselves quite
Ordinary

But God
Is never stopped
By that

When we give Him
Our "Yes!"
To be His hands…
To be His voice…

Through us
What He does
Cannot be called
Ordinary

That brings joy to my heart

Because

Well…
I'm ordinary

And I said…
"Yes!"

September 5, 2020

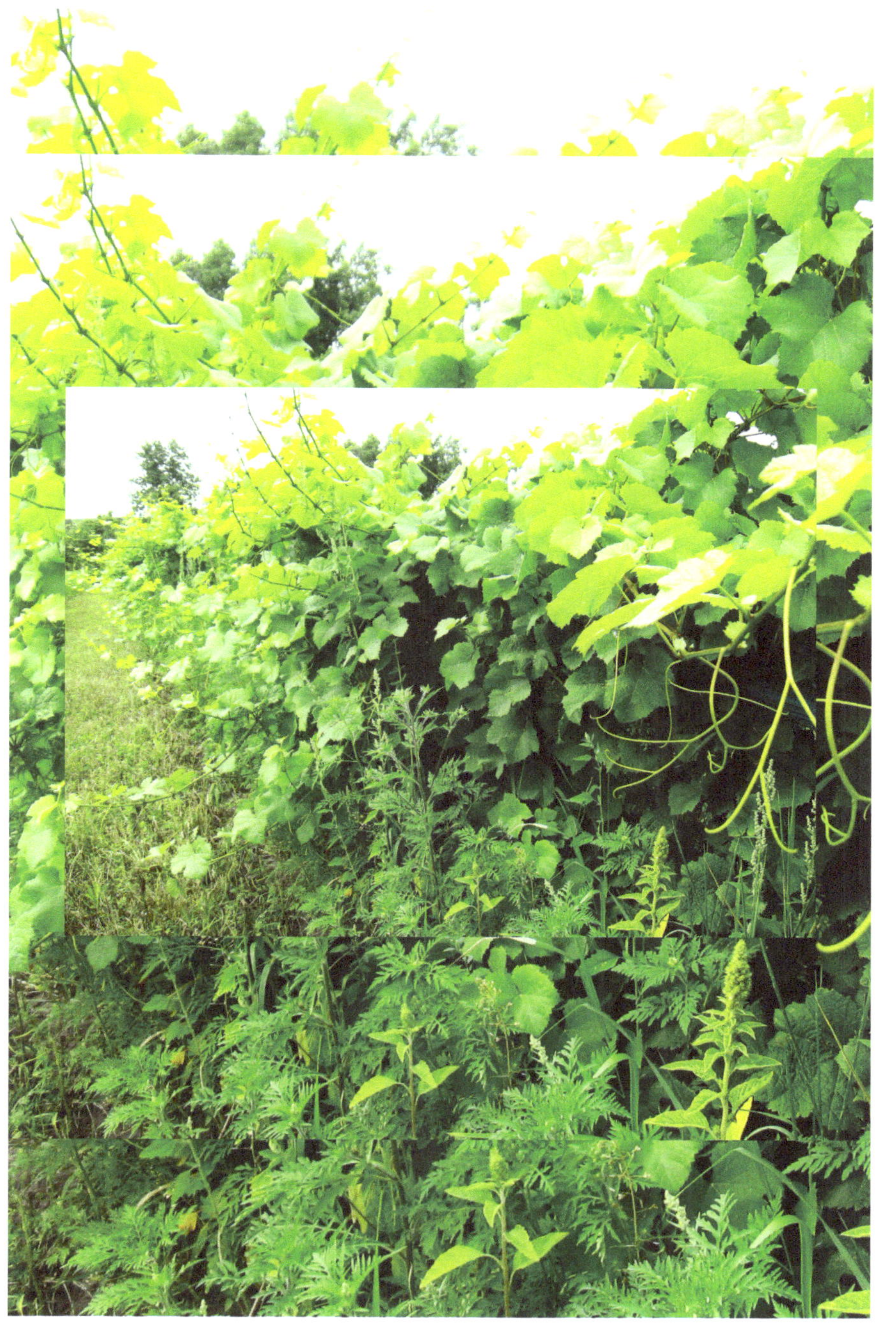

You take the floor away

Sometimes

You take the floor away

All that is left

Is a wire

We look up
And we see

We have no parachute

The things we wrongly relied upon
Are no longer here

We didn't realize
Our trust was divided

But You knew

So that's why

You take the floor away

To stop the division
To have us
Solely rely on You

We start walking

The wire is narrow
So we fall

But each time
You catch us

And each time
Our trust in You
Grows

September 9, 2020

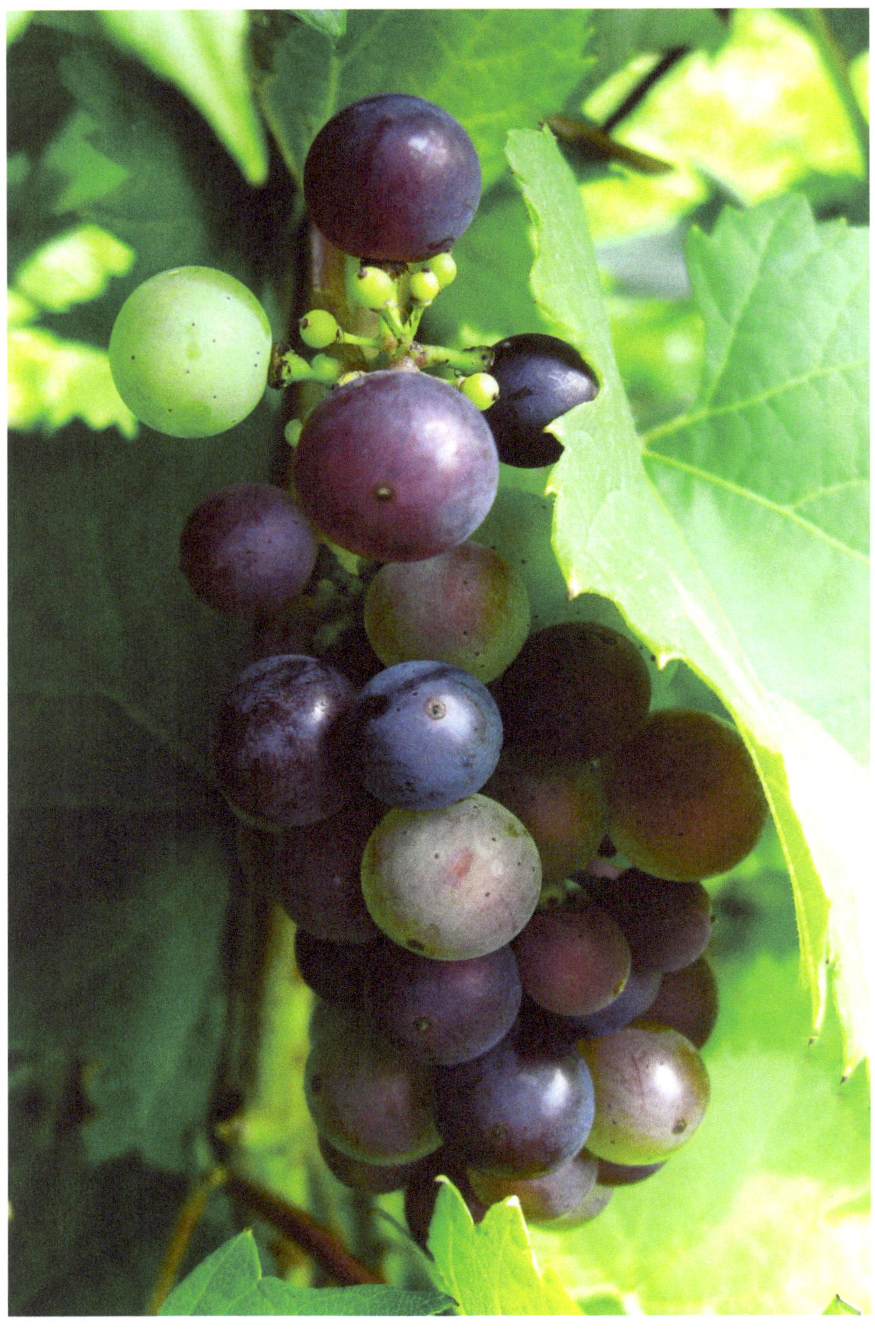

God lifts the veil

The Bible teaches us
There is a time to plant
And there is a time for harvest

We don't always see
The harvest from our planting
When we sow in someone else's life

But occasionally...
God lifts the veil
And we see

The changed life
Of the one we helped
A few months back

An encouraging word we spoke
That took time
To sink in
Did touch and lift someone's heart

Oh! How bless we are to see these harvests

Life can be so difficult

Keep planting, in faith
It always produces a good harvest
Whether you see it or not

And occasionally

God lifts the veil

And we see such beauty...

September 27, 2020

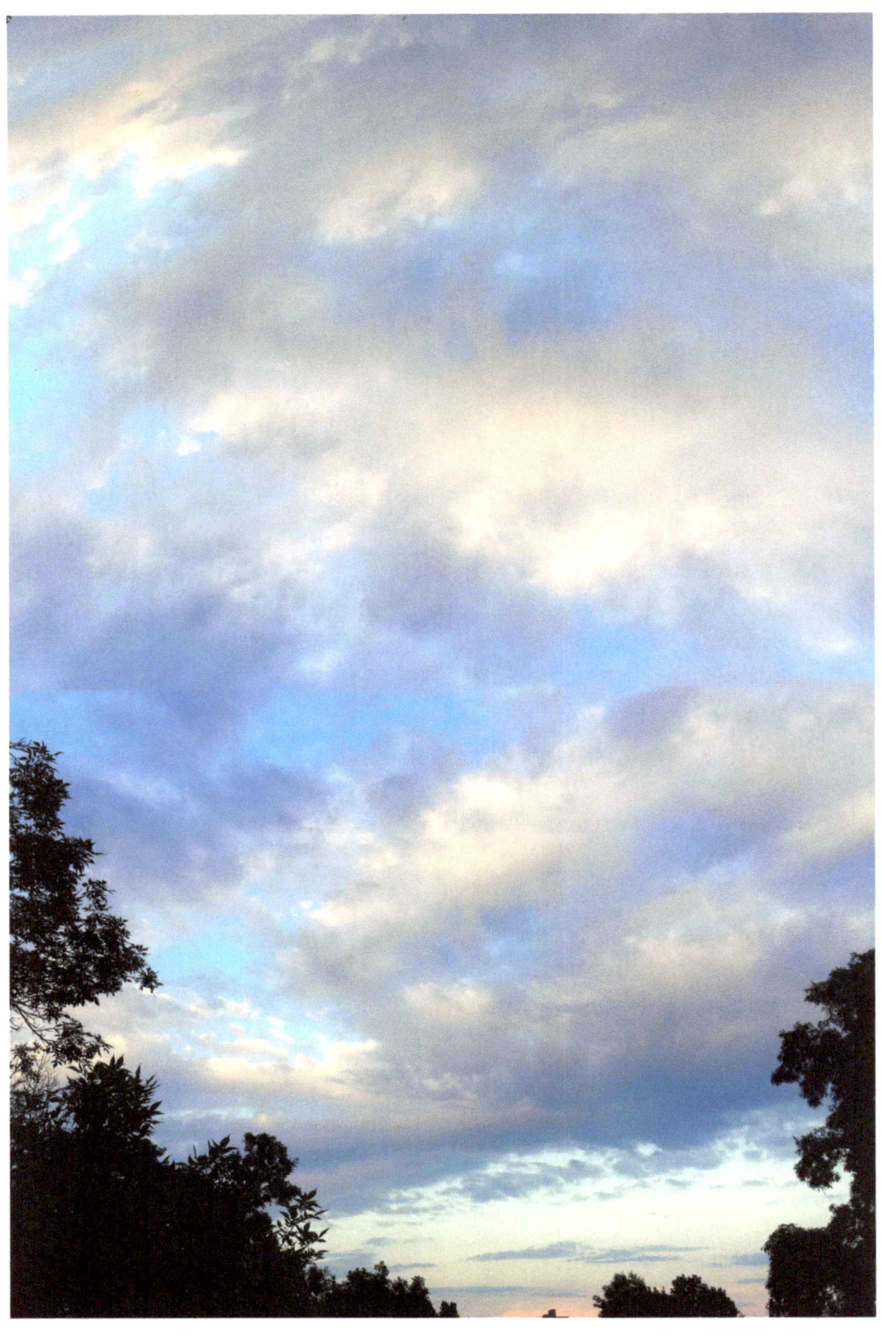

A handful of cloud

Pink
Blue
"Which colour would you like?" she asks

Big brown eyes
Staring
Nose to the glass

He looks up
"Blue. Please, Mama!"
"Alright!" she smiles

Then she nods at the man
And the rounding begins

The fluffy layers slowly increase
On the paper

Soon, it's ready

The boy reaches and grabs
A handful of cloud

The treat melts in his mouth

Cotton candy

A spiral of sugar thin lace
Delicate
Light

A sweet blue cloud
On a paper cone

September 28, 2020

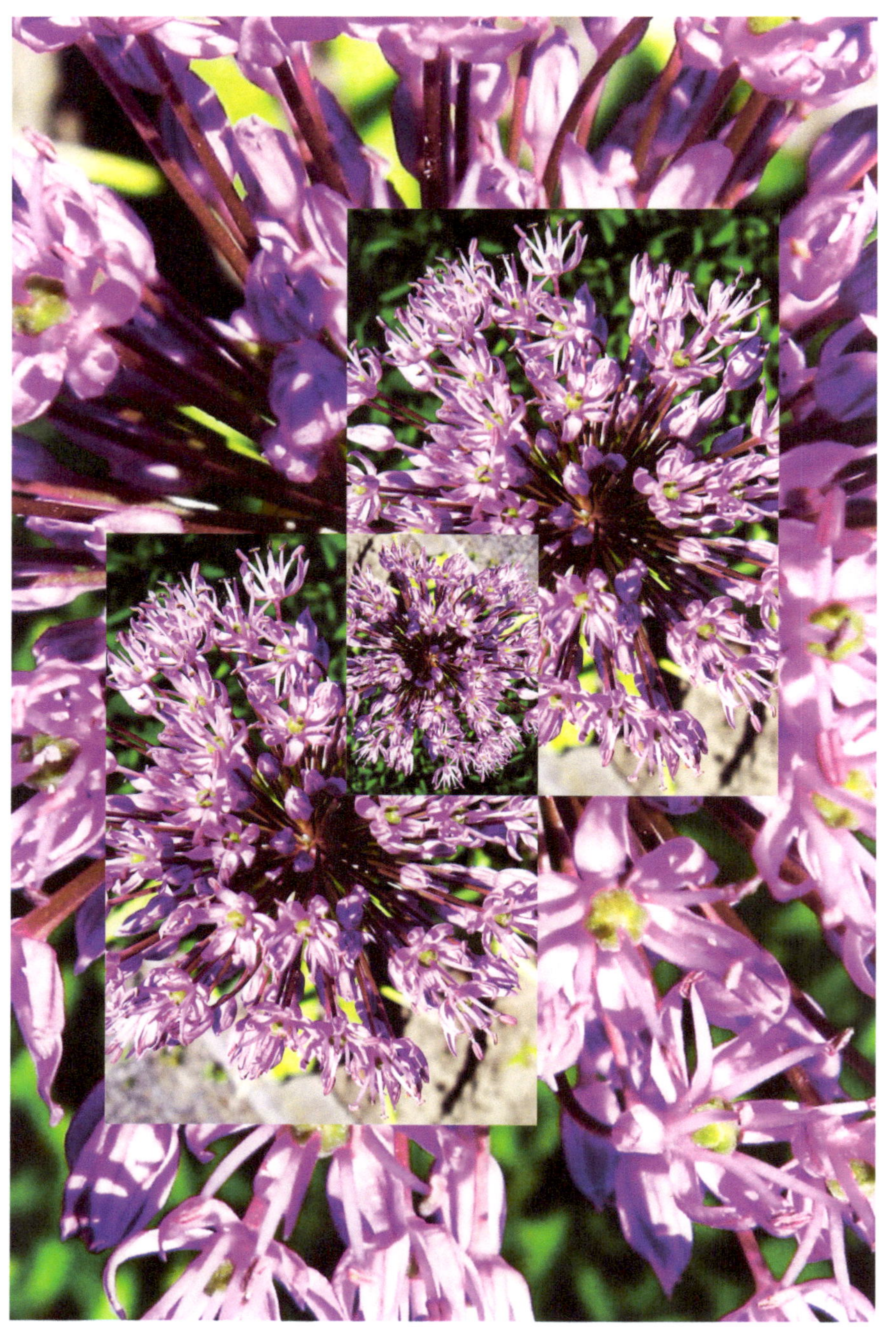

Dust

Dust...
Dust is everywhere...

It's on the floor...
It's on our streets...

We sweep it out
It creeps back in

It's an endless circle

We don't like dust...

But did we forget?

That's what we are
Well...part of it

Without God's breath of life in us
We're dust

Now I would imagine that

When God created the first man
The dust in that perfect world
Must have been
Quite different
Compared to
What we have here
In this fallen world

Nevertheless, even from gold
Even magnificent
Dust remains lifeless

God opposes the proud
But gives grace to the humble

Remembering that...
We come from dust

And, even if
It would still be
Stunning dust from a perfect world

We depend on God for life and for everything

Remembering that...
Helps us in our fight
To stay humble

Fight?
Yes...

Because
Pride...
Also tries to creep in

October 17, 2020

During the night

They came
During the night
Without a sound
Like little thieves

Invading the ground and the streets
Rooftops and chimneys

Slowly
Quietly

Some got caught in the wind
And started dancing among the trees

Then everything became
A little brighter

Something changed

The children saw them first
Early the next day

Peeking through the curtain
Suspecting before seeing
That it was...

A little whiter
Outside

The first snowflakes
Had arrived

Tiny ice crystals
Waltzing down
During the night
Without a sound

Slowly
Quietly

Covering the ground and the streets
Rooftops and chimneys

Draping the scenery
With a majestic white robe

And the children smiled
So eager to go play

In the glistening white snow
Sparkling in the sun

The snow that came...

During the night

November 3, 2020

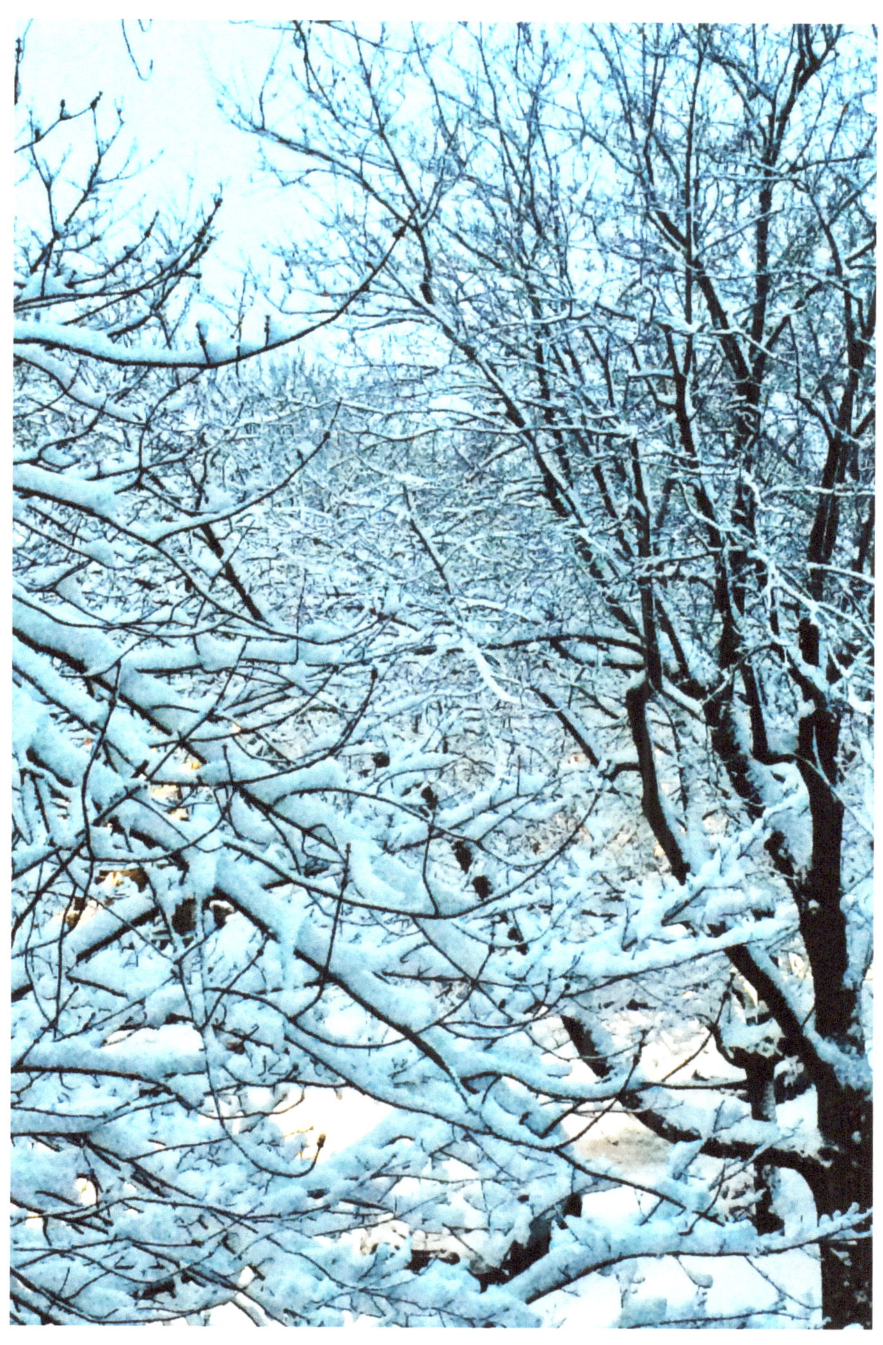

"And they lived happily ever after."

"And they lived happily ever after."

Famous ending of children's stories

So many things
Are different in the real world

No enchanted forest
No fairies
No magic wands...

And the heroes in most of these tales
Will encounter malevolent characters once

One episode, one battle to win the war
Between good and evil
To reach the "Lived happily ever after." part

How many battles do we face in a lifetime?
Too many to count
Certainly, a number
Miles and miles away from one
If you lined them all up in a straight line

Yes! Many things
Are different in the real world

Except one

The end

The one thing in common
With a fairy tale

You see, the winner
Of the final battle
Has already been declared

Jesus wins
Against Satan

We know the outcome
We know the end
It is written in the Bible

"And they lived happily ever after."
Will happen

I'd rather have
That certainty
Than one wish granted
By a story book genie

Even three

November 9, 2020

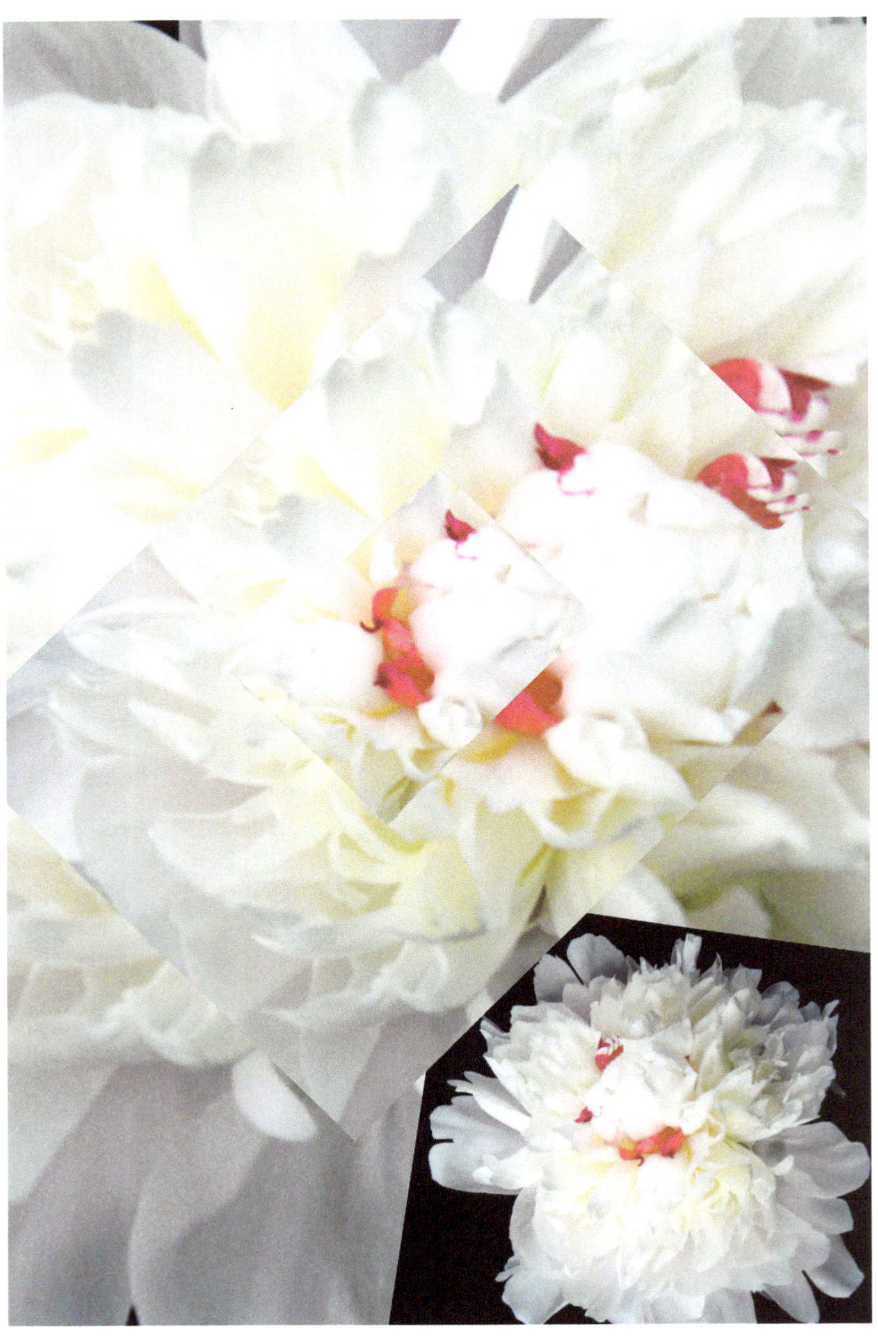

Gems in Heaven

There is a room in Heaven
Or so I imagine

Where God keeps
All our gems

As Jesus taught us
To store treasures in Heaven
There must be a room
Where they are kept

A spacious hall
Abounding with chests
Lids fully open
Overflowing
With colourful gems

Every time we do the right thing
A sparkling treasure appears in Heaven

We forgive an offence
We extend grace and mercy to others
More gems in Heaven

Did God draw a treasure map for each of us?
A map we don't see in advance?
It unfolds day by day
One hidden treasure at a time
For us to discover

I think so...

When God designed our life
He prepared, beforehand
Good works
For us to do

And each time
We choose to do them
These good works become...

Gems in Heaven

November 23, 2020

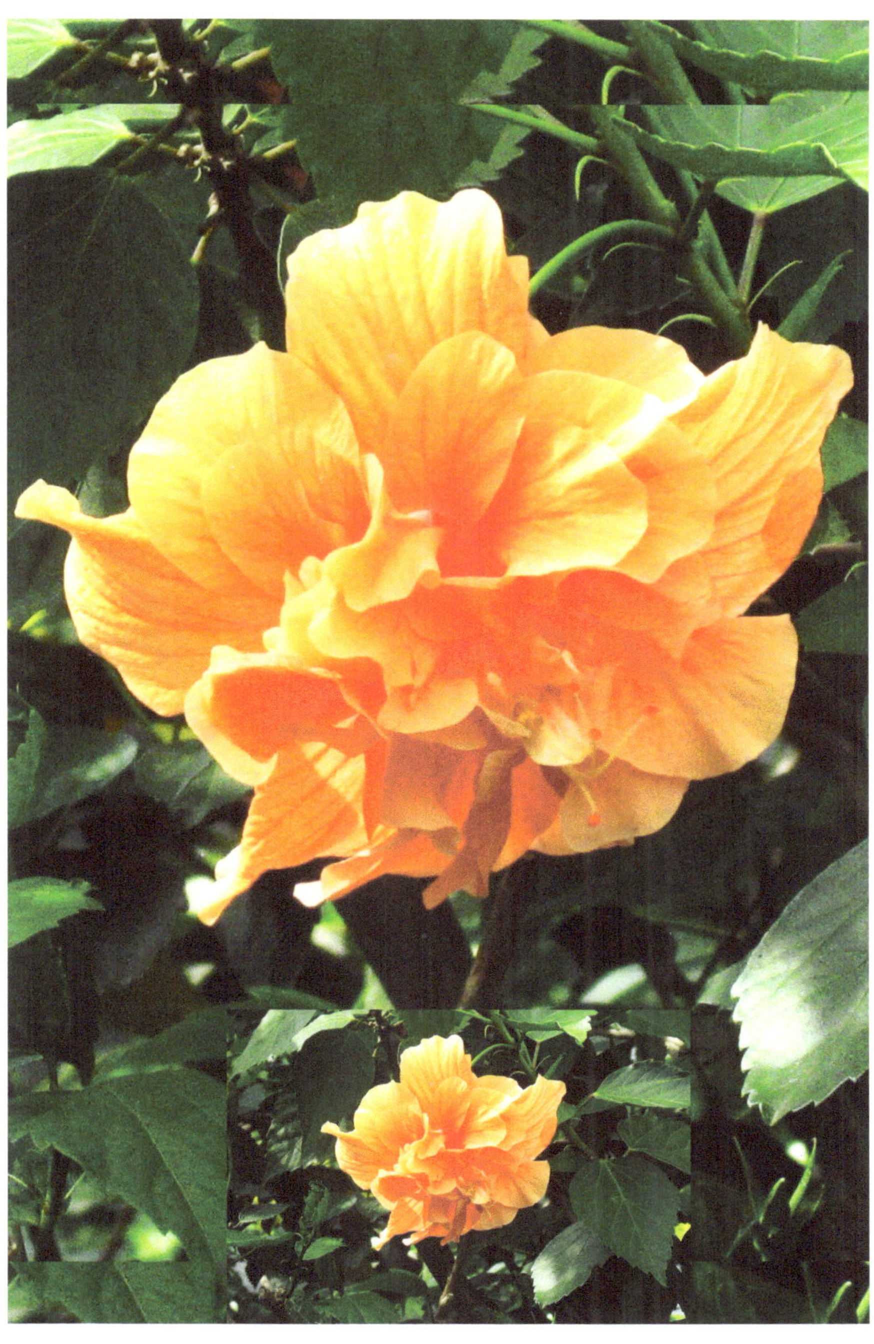

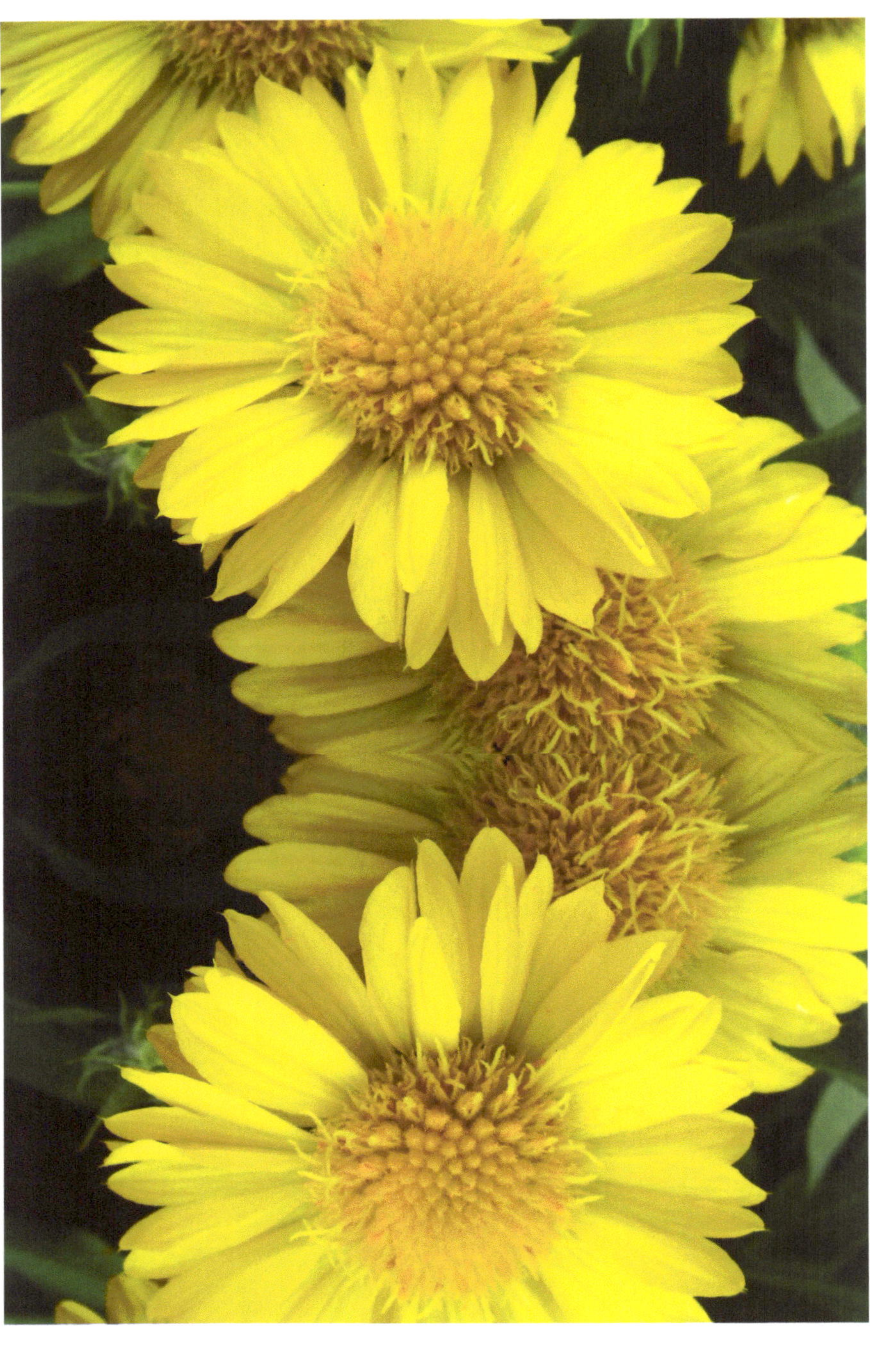

Time and its distant cousin

Time...

Did you notice
That time seems to have
A mind of its own?

These invisible little wheels
In the background of our lives
Don't pay much attention
To what we would like

They never stop or slow down
Change direction
Or increase their turning
No matter what we ask

But they are deceiving
Don't you think?

Test them...
Start having fun and see...

They become illusionists
And time...starts flying

To be fair
I will admit to their generosity
That occurs every four years

We do get a gift
Of an extra day

But honestly...
What we really want
Is a little bit
Of friendly cooperation
From time to time

"Would you forget to turn for a few hours?
Or secretly slow down
Extend this present moment
It is quite pleasant right now
Could you please?"

I tried
I was polite
It still fell on deaf ears

Or maybe their timing is off

Because, let me tell you
Anytime I'm waiting
They seem to remember my request from previous days
And then, they start acting
Just like little snails

Mischievous wheels

What a strange sense of humour they have

Kind of the same one I get
From their uncooperative distant cousin...

You know...

The other deaf one...

The weather

November 27, 2020

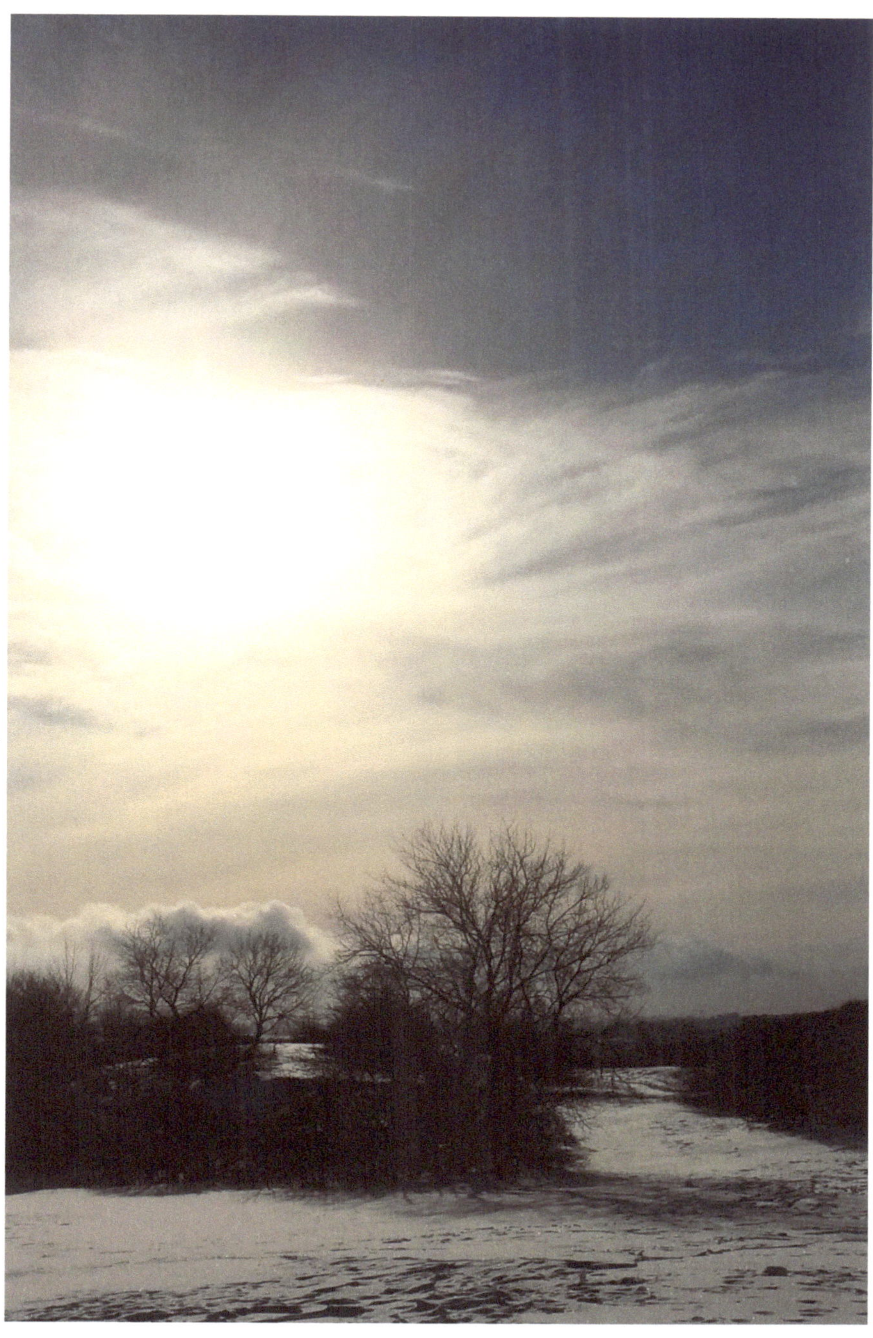

Where God is not there

God is omnipresent
In Heaven
On Earth

Yet, there is a place
Where God is not there

Hell

Perfect absence from God

A place totally without...

Love
Forgiveness
Joy
Help
Justice
Peace
Hope
Self-control
Kindness...

Never...not even for a second
And it never ends

Earth is for a given time
It has seasons of difficulties, pain, sorrow, trials, tribulations...
But they don't last forever
And God is there
With everything He represents

Now, imagine the opposite...

God made a way
For us
To never go there

We are to...
Keep the faith
And follow God's plan

Jesus went to prepare a place for us
So that we will
Always be with Him
Where He is

Choose the narrow gate
To never go
Where God is not there

December 4, 2020

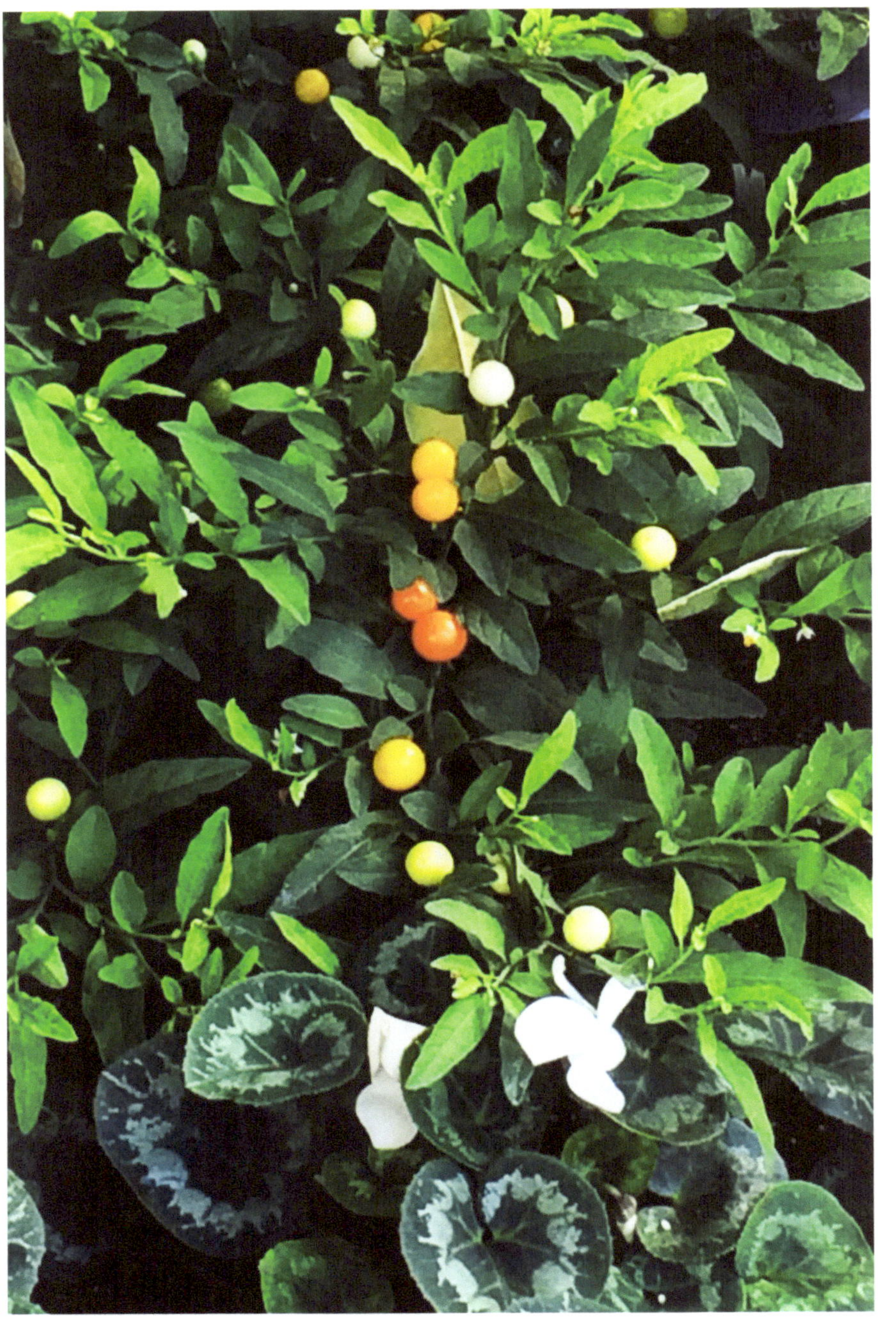

Sometimes...

I remember a day
Back in grade school
When I was taught
And hopefully...
So was the rest of the class
Something more than just math

The teacher had drawn
Three circles and a dot
On the big blackboard
A problem, an enigma
That she wanted us to solve

I was sitting as always
Way off in the back
Liking the remoteness
Provided by
The very last desk

I didn't raise my hand
I didn't say a word
But I venture
That the teacher must have seen
An expression on my face

She invited me to come
Way up front
Stand next to the board
To explain and to write
The solution that came up
That popped up in my head

As it turned out
I had found the correct answer
To the problem, the enigma
Of the three circles and the dot

I was also...
The only one
In the whole class

What the teacher did next
Is something I never forgot
Even after all these years

She used what had occurred
To teach me
And the rest of the class
A life lesson, more valuable than math

Sometimes...
You will be the only one who is right

A lesson in self-assurance
Meant to build confidence
And self-esteem in a small child

Not in a bragging way
Not in a proud way
On the contrary

Yes, we tend to assume
That a great multitude of people
When saying the same thing
Would automatically be right
Because there are so many of them
How could they be wrong?

And yes, sometimes they will be correct in their thinking

But other times...

It may not be the case

Don't lose trust
In what you are thinking

Don't quickly dismiss it
Just because it's only you
The crowd is not always right

Sometimes...
You will find yourself
To be the only one
Who is actually right

December 9, 2020

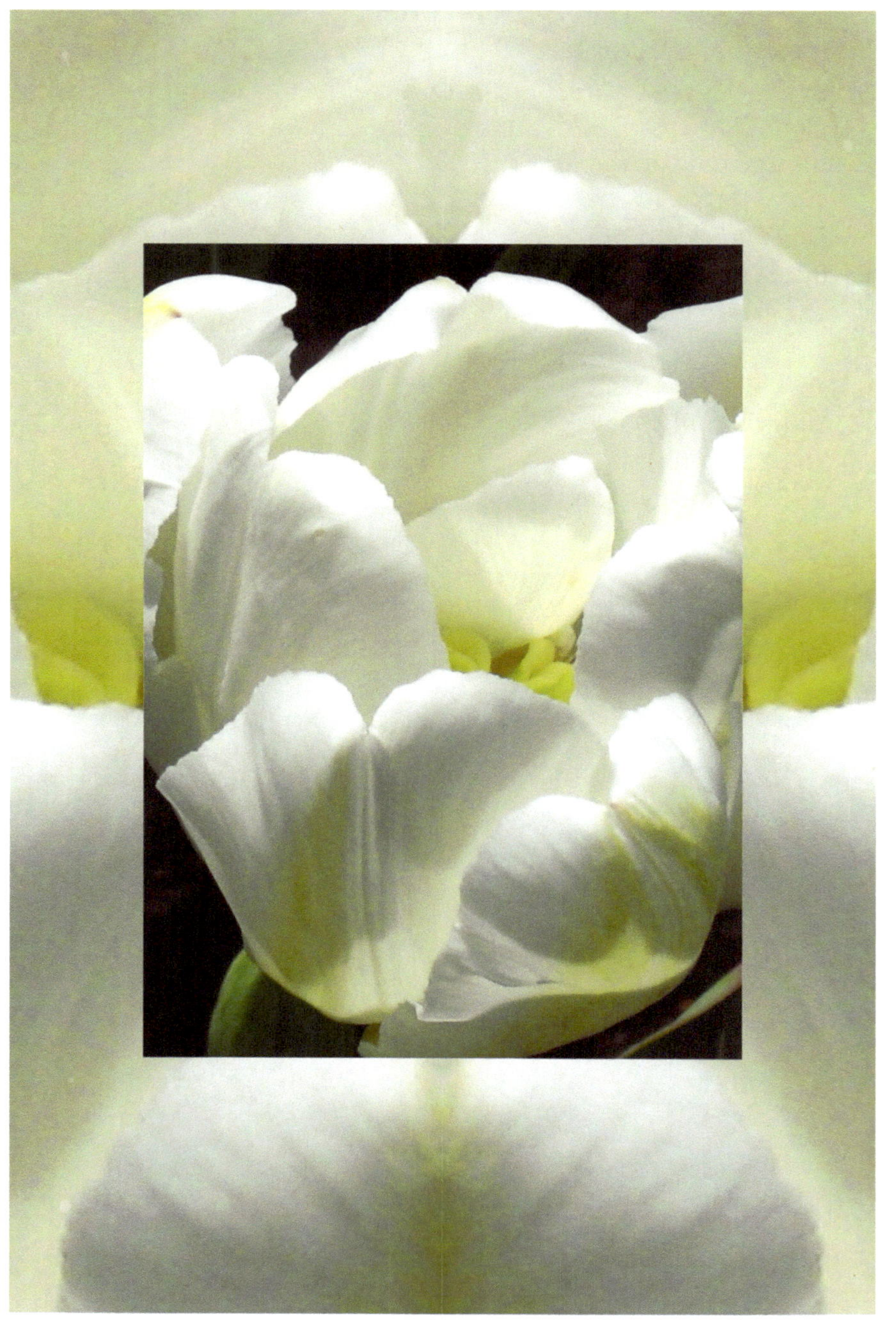

Promises...

Promises...

Like fragile vases
Handle them with care

They are entwined
With trust
And feelings
That exist
Between the giver
And the believer

Promises...

Neglect or break too many of them
You will see that...

Trust cracks and avalanches itself away

Feelings...
Tarnished with hurt
Are turning colder

The relationship...
Or what is left of it
Is now between an untrustworthy one
And a no longer believer

Promises...

When never kept
Are only entwined
With cold unbelief

Don't let them be
Empty vases

Give them with care

Give them with intent

December 17, 2020

Did You know?

When You were growing
In Mary's womb
Did You know?

When You rested
In the manger
Did You know?

When obedient parents
Kept You safe
Did You know?

When You saw shapes and colours
For the first time
Through human eyes
Did You know?

When You were a child
Learning how to walk
Did You know?

Before the age of twelve

Jesus...

Did You know?

That...

You are the Son of God
You are the Word
You created it all

Did You know back then?

I believe You did
Then
Now

Always

The Father, the Son, and the Holy Spirit
They are all One
God in three Persons

God is All-Knowing

Always

December 24, 2020

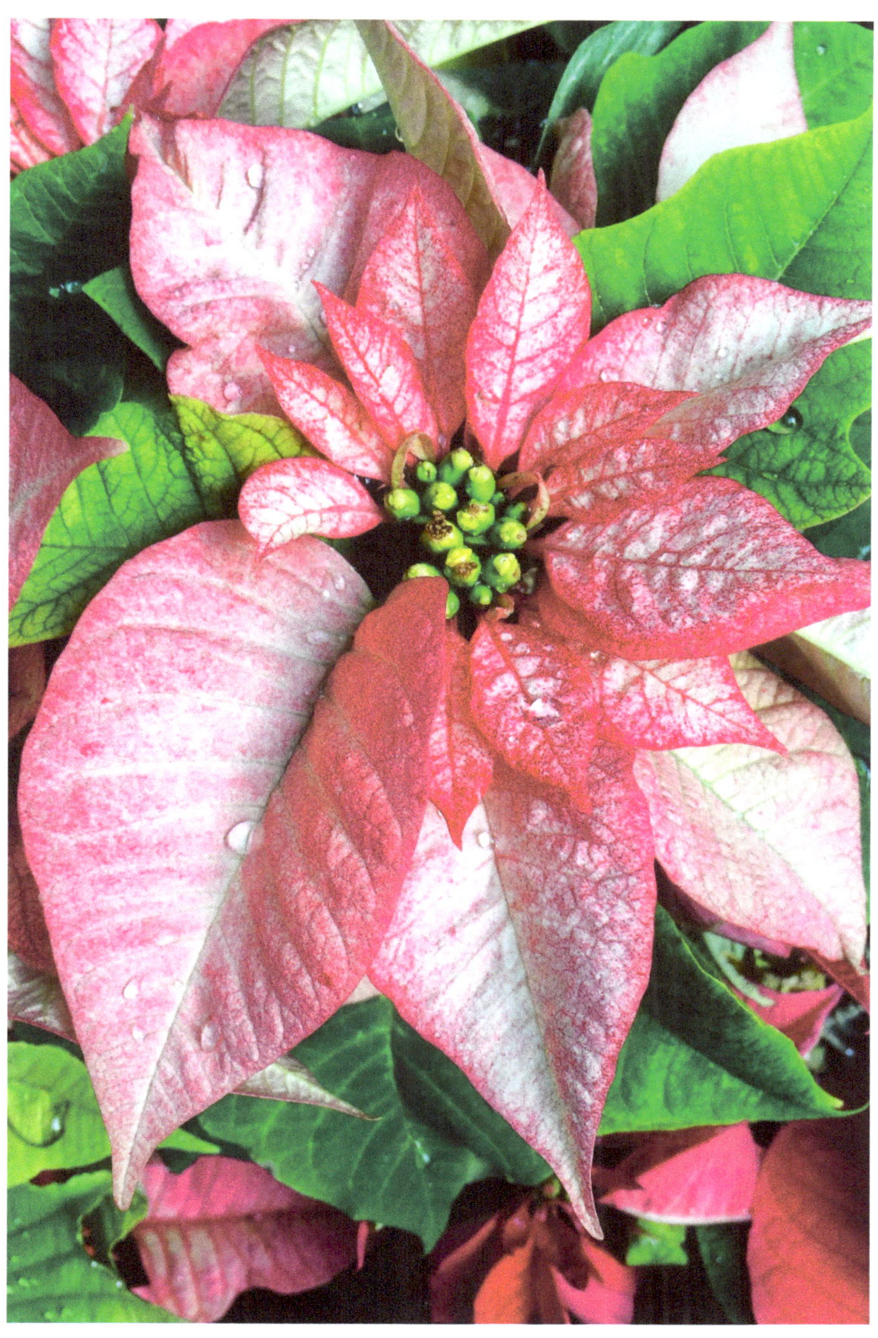

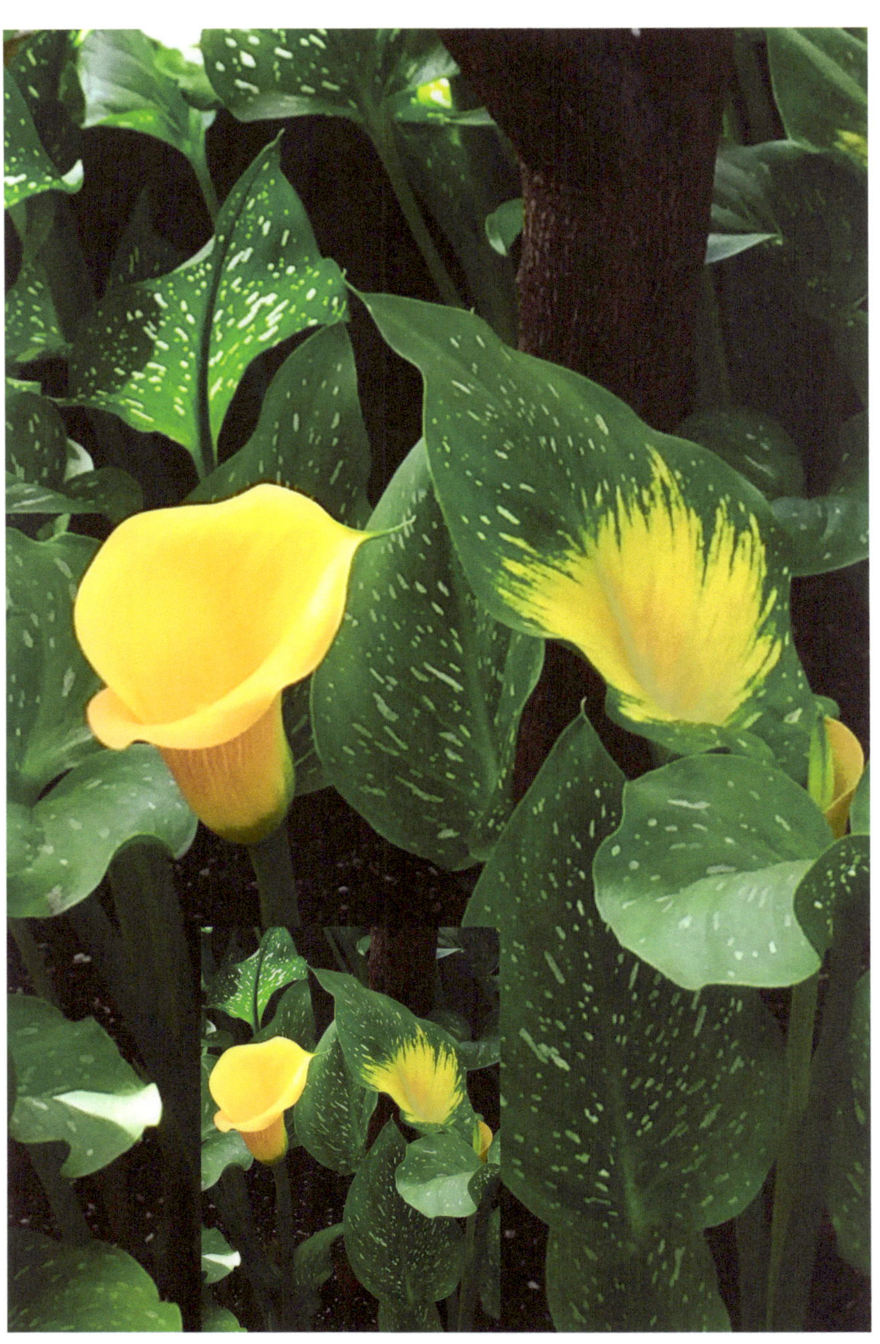

Clowns...

Clowns...

Artists with
Emotions painted on their faces
Happy or sad

Once the makeup is done
They stopped having a choice

Which way
The exaggerated fake mouth corners
Are turned
Determined their moods

Yet who can tell
How they really feel inside

Hiding their feelings while performing
Is harmless
To clowns

What about in real life?
When there is no make believe

I did that once

I needed to grieve
But I didn't

At the time
The sadness I felt
Didn't seem justified
So I brushed it off
And focused on other things

I accomplished a dream
I never had time before

That was good

The brushing off
Was not

A few months later
Something triggered
The hidden sadness
To surface

Unaddressed
It had grown

I grieved then
Vowing to myself
Never to dismiss again

Feelings are to be addressed
Not ignored

Make believe
Is for clowns

Sooner or later
The makeup will crack
And you will need to deal
With how you really feel inside

January 8, 2021

Success

Success...

Seven letter word
With a million definitions

Everyone seems to have their own
Don't they?

As far as the world is concerned
It views success
In a very shallow way

Outer beauty
Wealth
Power
Influence...

What a tiring life that is
Always working
To hold on to
Success
With things that don't last

Eventually
You will fail
Then what?

Don't use the world's scales
To measure success

People are more than just...

The skin they live in
Financial sheets
Or career status

Raise your eyes

Embrace
God's definition of
Success

At the end of my life
I want to hear Him say:

"Well done, good and faithful servant!"

What could possibly
Matter more
Than having
Eternal life
With Him
In His Kingdom?

One day
The world
As we know it
Will cease to exist

Everything will be made new!
Everything will be perfect!

Oh!
Did you pay attention?

The world...
Just like the things
It values
Will cease to exist one day

So why should you care
What it thinks
About...

Success

January 12, 2021

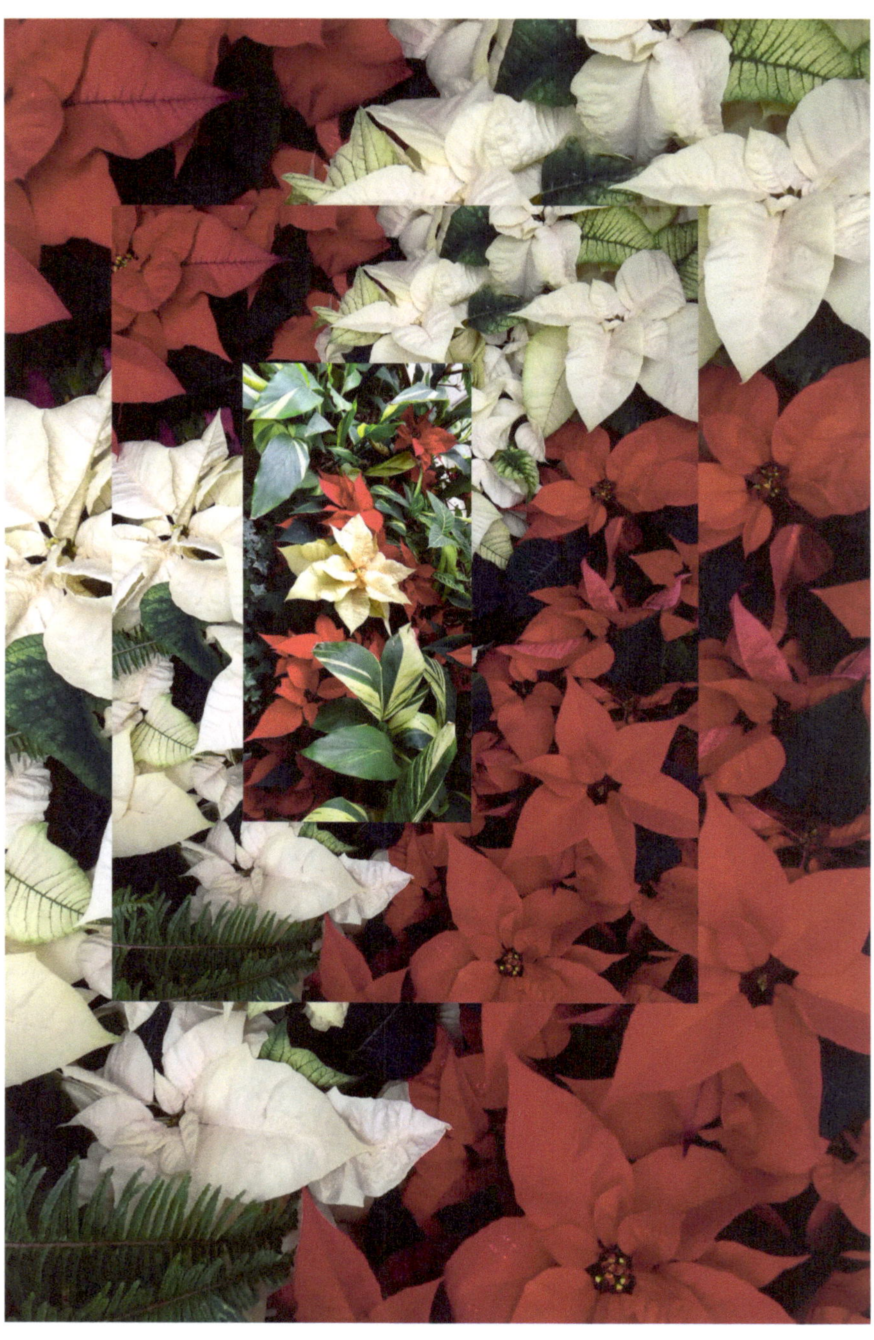

Don't

When you store away the decorations
Don't put Christmas in a box

Don't stuff it there
With the red suit
And the lights

It doesn't belong there

You can't contain it in a box
It's so much bigger than that

And it's not
A once in a year thing

It is meant
To live in our grateful faith-filled believing heart
Every day

Christmas is a precious gift from God
A loving, unselfish, willing redemption act starting with
The Word becoming human
It's Jesus saying yes, agreeing to do that

It is a doorway
That God opened more than two thousand years ago
It's the only door that truly matters in life

Without Christmas
There is no Easter

Without Easter
There is no one in Heaven

Without Christmas
There is no Easter
There is an overcrowded hell

Is that what you want to store away in a box?
And forget about it the rest of the year

Don't

Do remove the decorations

Leave the dry tree
On the side of the road
For the city's pickup

Take down the lights from outside your home

But don't...

Extinguish
At the same time

Christmas...
From your heart

January 29, 2021

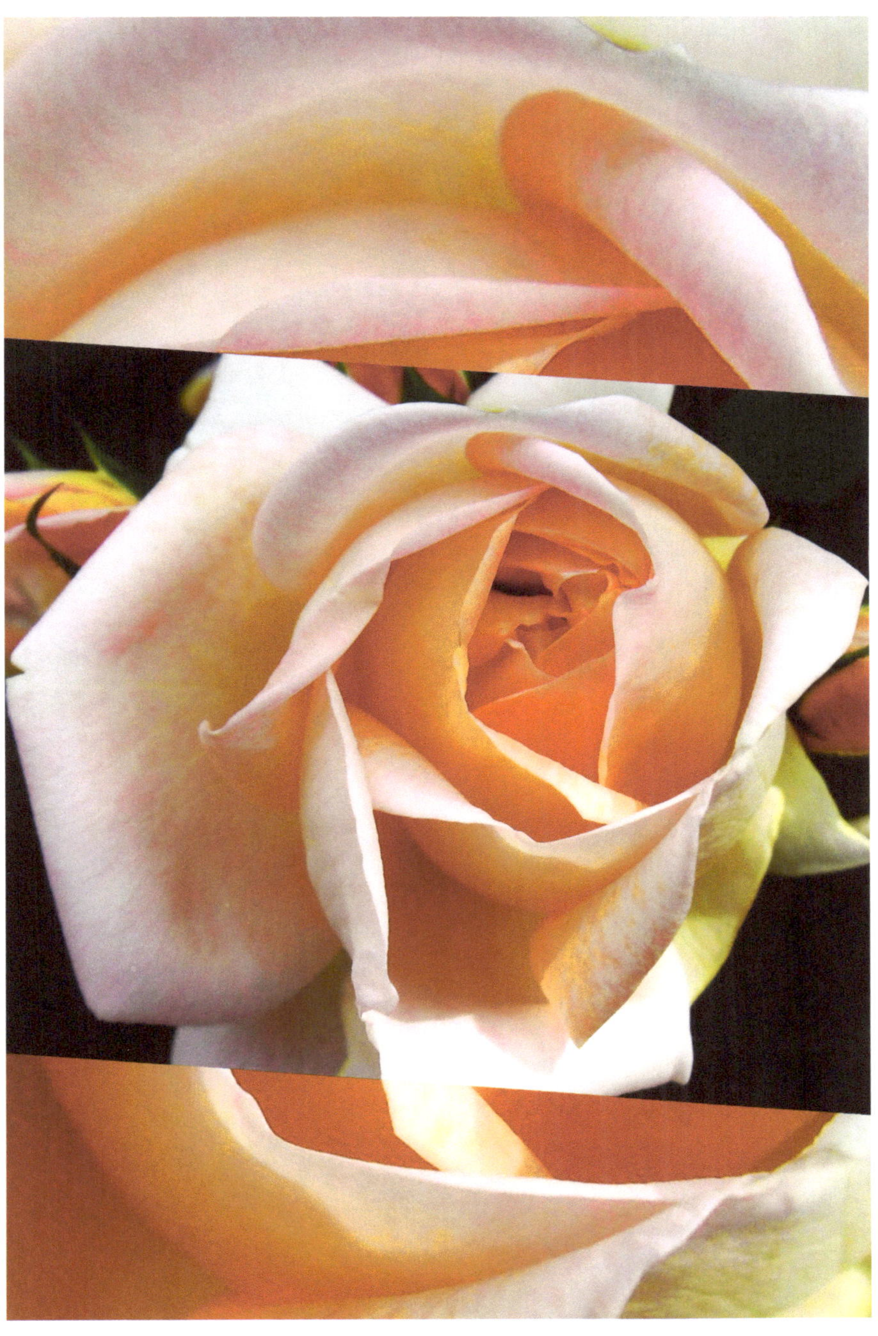

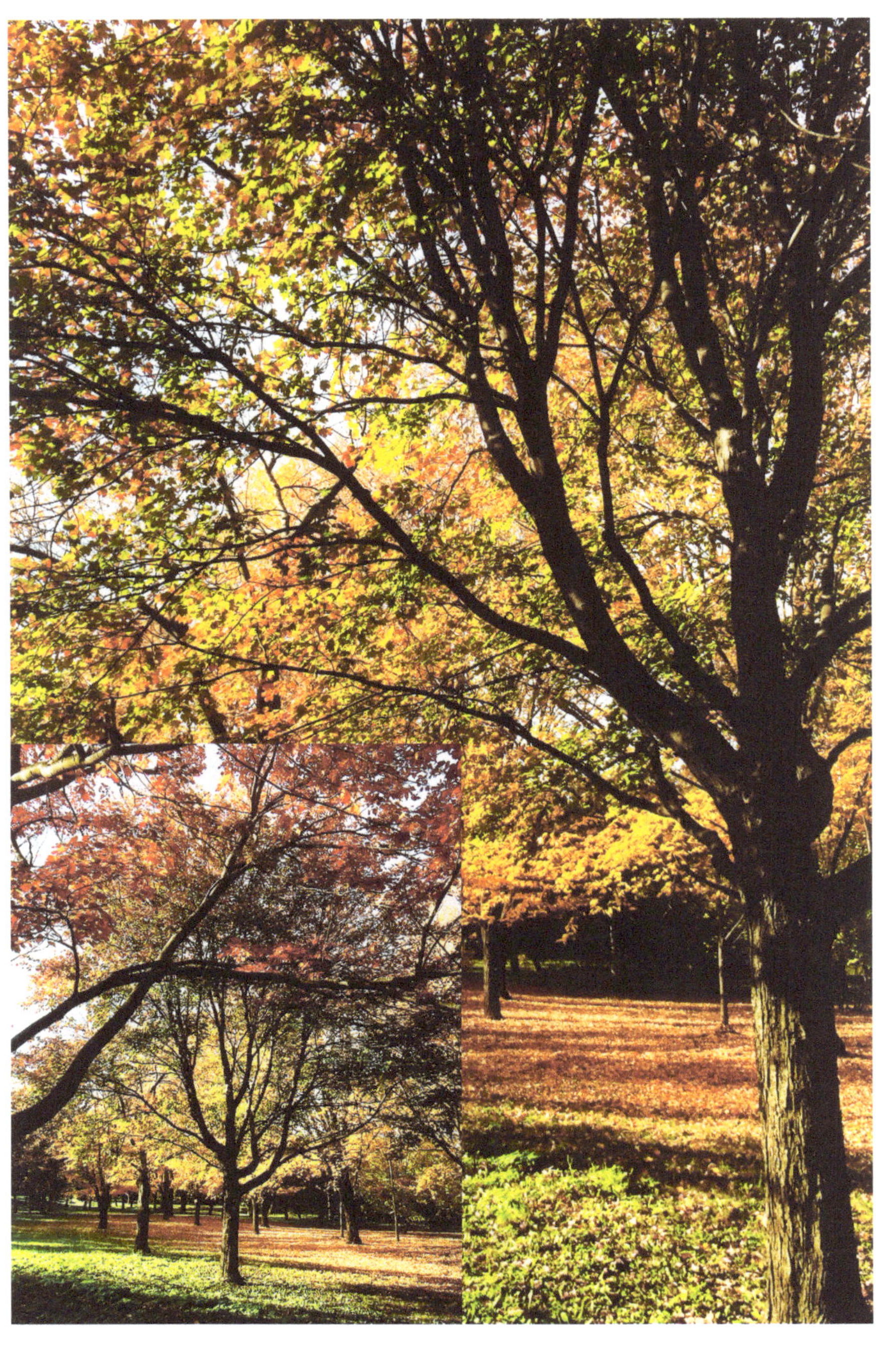

Rusty and Angel

Rusty
Curled up on a stump
Didn't hear the sound
Of the rustling leaves

Angel
Wanted to see the stars

Earlier today
She found the perfect tree
With lots of criss-crossing branches
Reaching for the sky

She made a nest
Close to the top
With fallen feathers and twigs
Then she settled for the night
And fell asleep
While gazing at the stars

We should all be like Angel
Pursuing our dreams
The dreams God put in our hearts

He gave us the abilities
The talents
The opportunities
To make them come true

We won't lack anything
But we need to do our part

It could be studying
Taking a leap of faith and changing our career
Or start a family even with all the uncertainties of life

It can take many forms
But we always have a part to play
It is not for passive people

Now back to our story

What is going on with Rusty?
Why is he there?
Looks passive to me

Well...

You see, the little chipmunk forgot
Her tendency to roll
In the middle of the night

So off she went tumbling down
Rustling the leaves
As she fell
From high up in the tree

He was there at the right place
To soften the blow

She landed on him like she would on a pillow

Angel knew the rust colour fox
He was her friend
But she never thought of sharing her dream with him

"I am sorry I woke you," she said
"I fell from the tree."

"What were you doing up there?" he asked
"Don't chipmunks sleep underground?"

"I wanted to see the stars."

"Oh Angel! I can help you,
I often sleep up there."

So off they went
And together
Angel accomplished her dream
With the help of her non-rolling friend
And never again
Fell from the tree

God places
Rustys in our lives

To help
Not get too hurt
As we fall

To not give up
And try again
When we do

To help us
Accomplish our dreams

Together
See the stars
Way up in the sky

In your life
You will be a Rusty
For a time

God will also call you
To be an Angel
To pursue your dreams

Don't let fear stop you
There will be a friend
If you fall

February 11, 2021

What do you long for?

What do you long for?

I long for joyful days that never end…

I long for a world where…

Pain and sadness
Are words that don't exist
For lack of use

If I forget to look both sides
Before I cross the street
I will never get hurt, or worse

Liars and thieves
Along with untrustworthy people
Selfishness
And evil intent
Are not allowed in

Negative thoughts
Never enter our mind
Controlling what we think about is no longer needed

We only think good things

I long for a world with…

The beauty of winter
Without the deadly cold
And the perilous ice

Long summer days
Without the scorching heat
And the sun burning our skin

Tornados and rising rivers
That are no longer destroyers of lives
They are just beautiful to see

Birds and animals
Not frightened by us
And us by them

What do you long for?

I long for Heaven

I long to see God face to face
And drown in His love

Have a two-way conversation
A very long one
With my Creator

See the Light and the Holy Spirit

Take a walk with Jesus in the cool of the evening

See those who are dear to me
That right now
I only see in my dreams

I long for...

The Eternal season to start...

What do you long for?

February 23, 2021

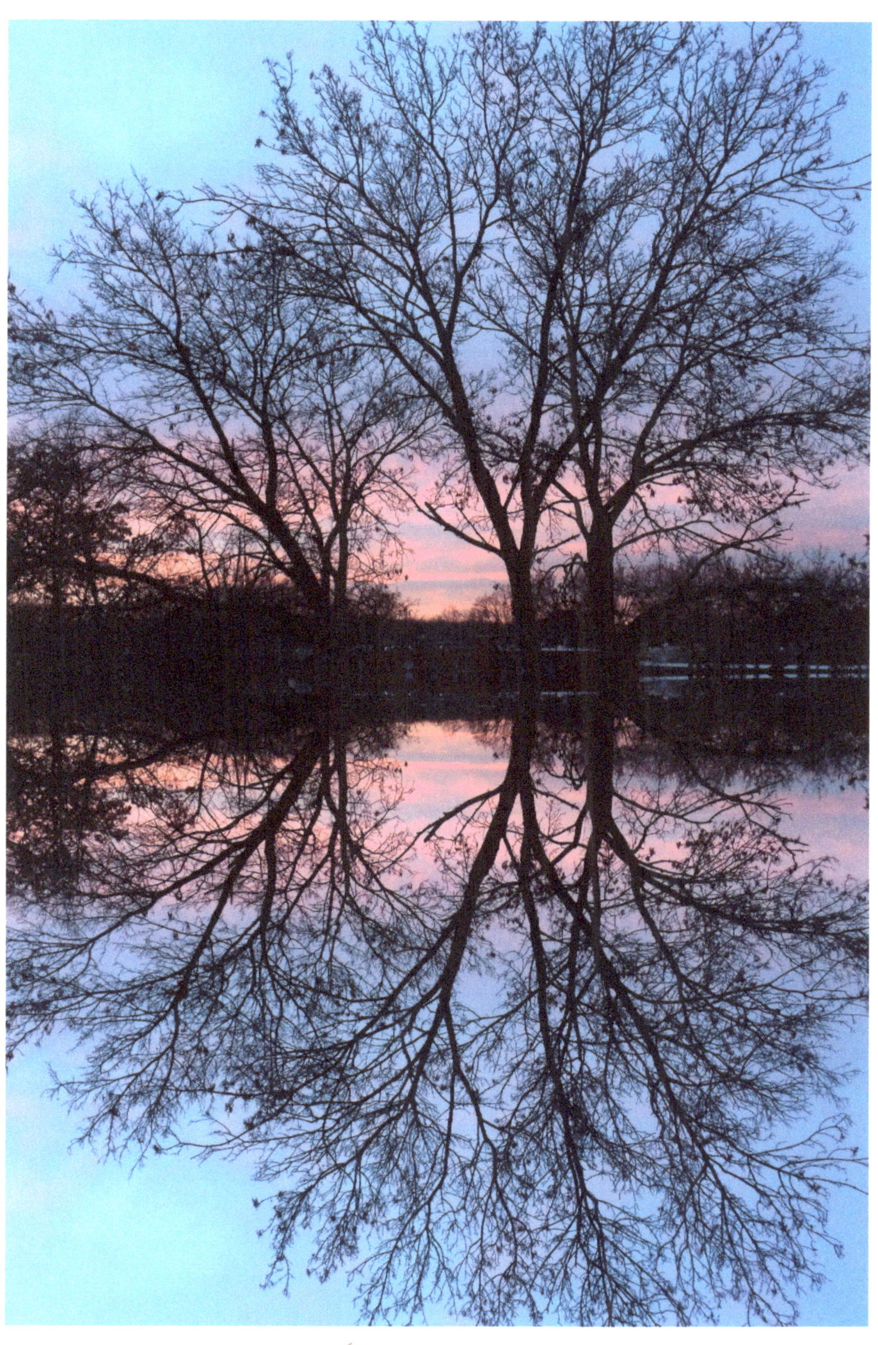

Until you...

February 27, 2021

Don't you know?

Saying you are sorry
But continuing
The same behavior
Nulls the apology

Don't you know?

Lacking consideration
Of others around you
Will eventually
Make them
Do the same

And walk away

Don't you know?

I guess we didn't go
To the same school

Did we?

God has been tugging
For me to let go
And let Him
Handle this

And so I shall

Until you graduate

I am walking away

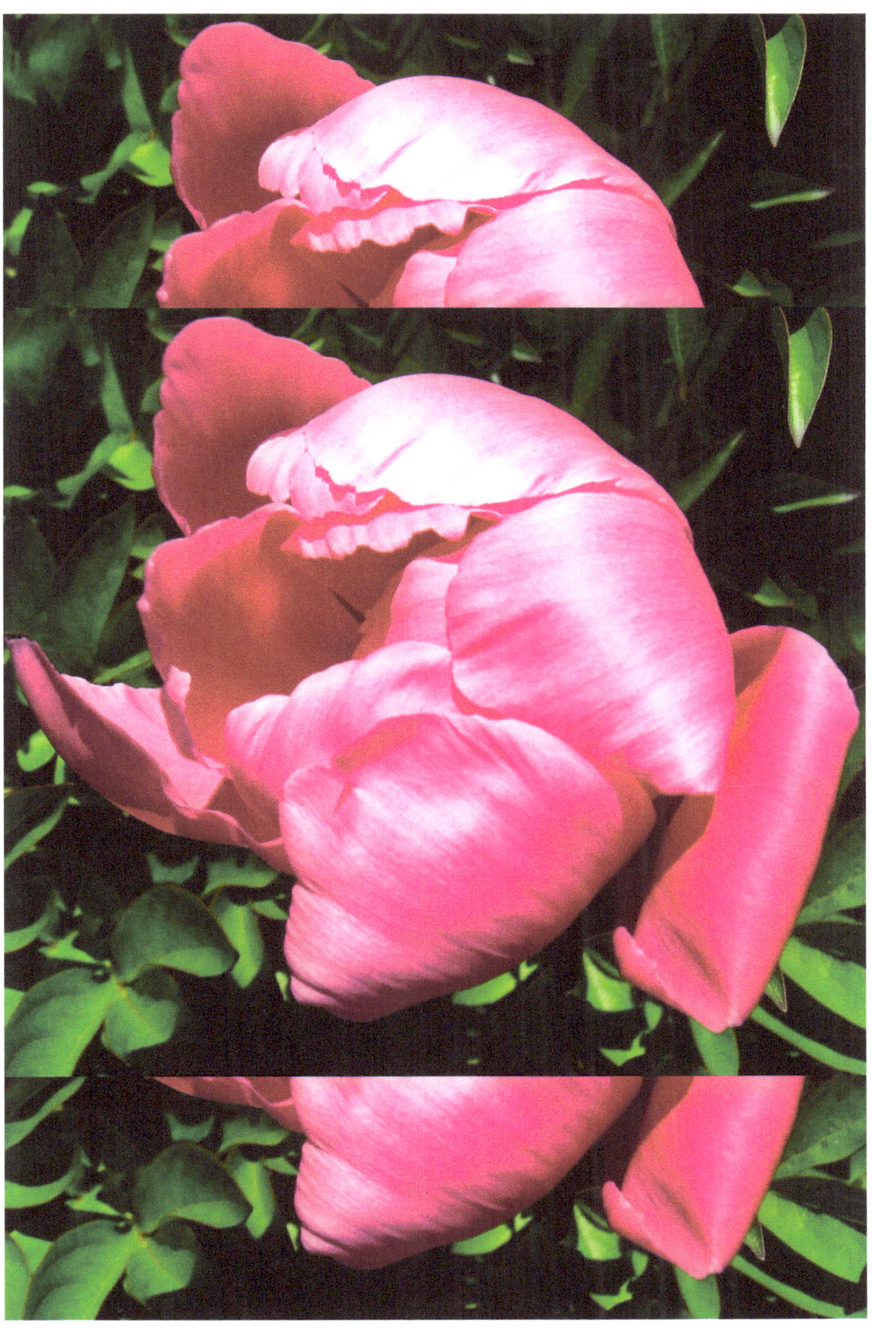

More than just...

Music...

There is something in it
That connects with our soul
Our emotions

I don't know how to explain it

How can a keyboard
A singer and a drum
Produce a sound
That vibrates in us?

A sound so joyful that we dance
So gentle that we feel tears
So powerful that we are moved

Even stirring up courage when we feel overwhelmed

What exactly is it touching
Inside of us
In our soul?

A few notes
And we are taken back in time
To a place in our past

What is that essence?
What is that component in music that does all that?

A song, a melody can lift our spirit
Wrap us up
In its wave
In its symphony

What exactly is it reaching
Inside of us?

Our Heaven part?

Is that why Jesus sang?

Did you miss that part too?
From the Bible

I did
Even though
I must have read it a few times

Oh how we read, but do not see!

But at the right moment
God does
With His way
Show us what we missed

A good friend, a pastor
Drew my attention to it

And there it was

It's in Matthew
Just after The Last Supper

"Then they sang a hymn and went out to the Mount of
Olives."

Jesus was with His disciples
And He sang with them

A song of praise to God

Why?

To go back in time
And immerse Himself in Heaven
Before the battle
In the Garden

To strengthen His Spirit
Over His flesh
To imagine Heaven without us
And say, "It cannot be."

To feel close to God
The Divinity
The perfect Unity He shared
With God and the Holy Spirit
Grab, like a drowning man, the Members of the Trinity
Before He had to let go and feel the separation
The Wrath of God
On the cross
If He chooses to

Drink in Their Power
Arm His soul with strength
And courage
To face the decision
The choice to give, or not
His life as payment for our sins

He knew the power of a song
He is the Creator
He created them all

He knows the power of a song
Especially one
That glorifies God

It's His Power!

That is what
Is in it

That is why it is so strong, so powerful, so soul grabbing...

That is why it does miracles!

So Jesus sang with His disciples...because He knew all that and
He needed it

May we remember to do the same

May we remember that we need it too

Make room in your life
For music
For singing

In the happy moments
To celebrate
To enjoy life

And also, and most definitely
In the tough times

To move you

To reach your soul

Your Heaven part

To lift your spirit

And give you courage

Always take time
To sing to God

To bring you
Close to Him

Tap into His Power

Jesus did

Jesus will sing with you...

And it will do more...

Than simply be...

Just...

A beautiful sound

March 18, 2021

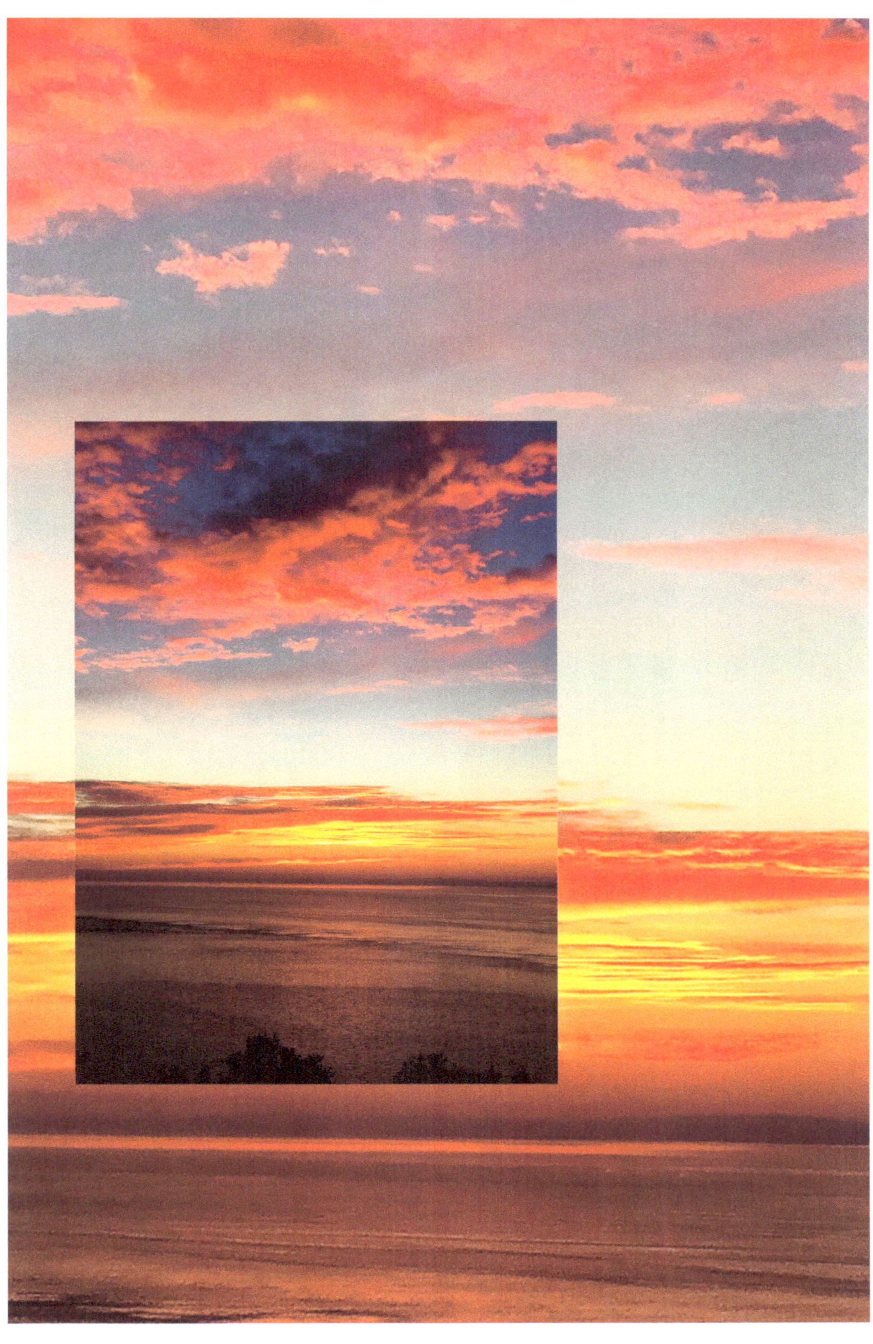

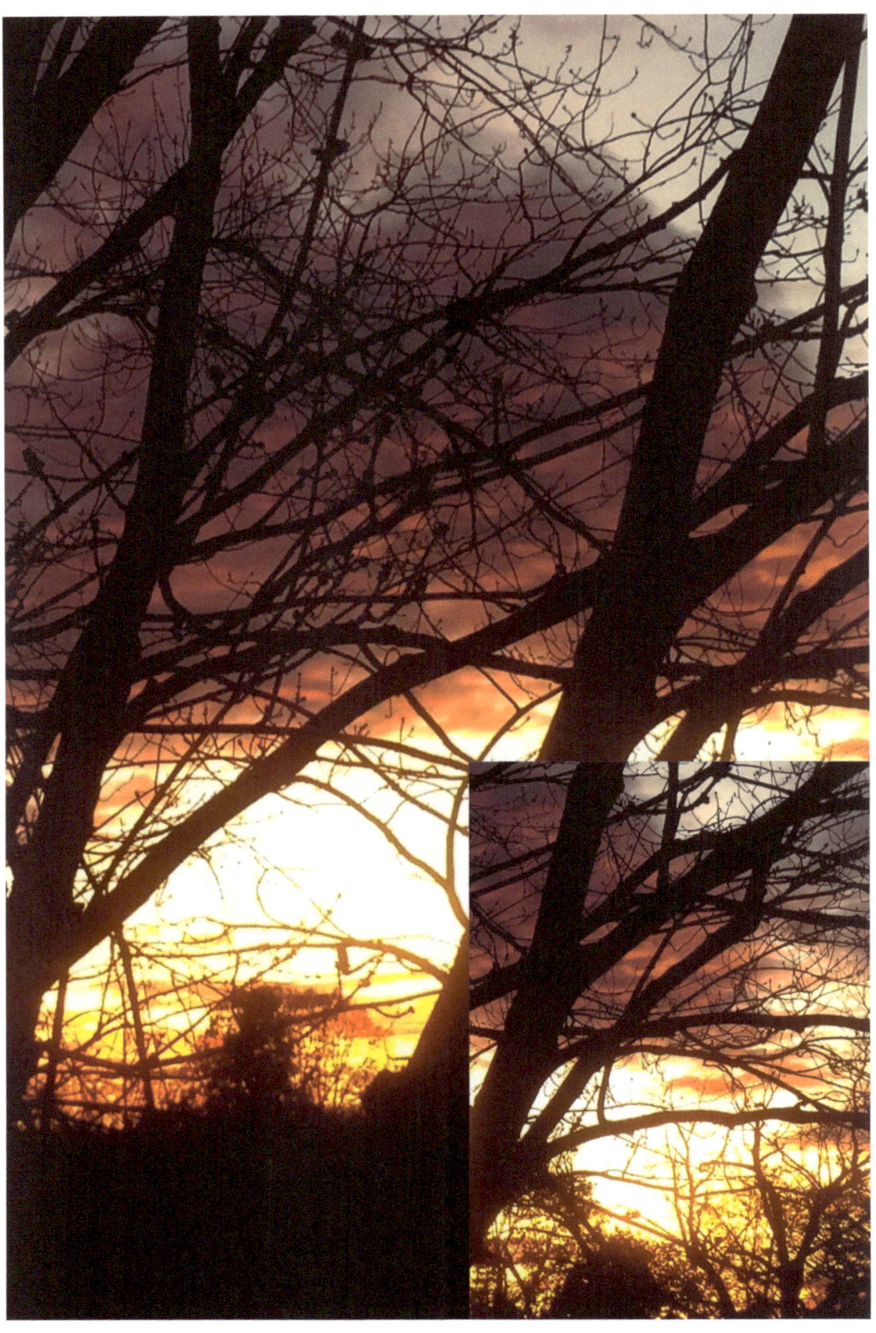

A war erupted

A war erupted
On a peaceful day

I saw the spinning trundling sleeves
Of the black and grey coat
As it rolled in
And covered the sky
All heavy with rage

The wind
Started banging on the window
Like it was trying to get in
Get away from the pouring tears
That had started to fall

Big water drops
Ran on the glass
Just like race cars would
Trying to win
A non-existing prize
Given to the first one
Who reaches the ledge

Fighting clouds
Exploded on gigantic drums
Suddenly blasting
Loud, causing near deafness
Bombing noises
Scaring everyone

Fire joined in
Shooting down
Zigzagging arrows with long tentacles
Temporarily blinding the sky
And burning the ground where they landed

Streets became little rivers
While the tantrum went on

Then suddenly...
The last bang was heard

The thunder
And the lightning
Stopped competing with each other

The wind
Dripping everywhere
Shook off
Its remaining wetness
Leaving huge puddles behind

My window stopped crying

The coat in the sky
Retracted itself
Revealing the sun
From its hiding place

A war had erupted...

But now peace has returned
And it came bearing gifts

The water and the sun
Creating magic

A spectacular rainbow
Suddenly appeared

Breathtaking colours
Arching closely together

Falling from the sky

March 26, 2021

Now!

Going through events
In your life
With someone you share a friendship with
Or love
Will bring you closer

The events can be
Joyful or difficult
The bonding comes from
The helping or supporting each other through it
Or partying together

You build memories
You share a history with one another

A bond is formed
And fortified, with time

Trust is established and grows
As well as the love or the friendship
With one another

Realistically
It will not be
The same person
Throughout your entire life

You will have...

Family
Friends
Coworkers
Neighbors...
The list goes on

But there is one
That shares everything

Absolutely
Everything
With you

There is nothing
You will ever do alone
No matter how you feel

There is no party
Where He won't happily go and dance with the group
Not a single one

Are you smiling?

You should...

He invented celebrations
Of course He wants to go with you
He loves you

And He also wants to do
The regular life with you
You know...
The days between events

You can do it all
With Him...

It's up to you...

The decision is yours
He will never force your hand

The invitation
Is on the table...

If you accept
He will make His home in your heart...

With Jesus as Your saviour, living inside of you
No relationship can ever be
Closer than that

Imagine the bond
The strength that ties you together
When you do
Everything with Him

Stop imagining it

Start living it...

Now!

April 3, 2021

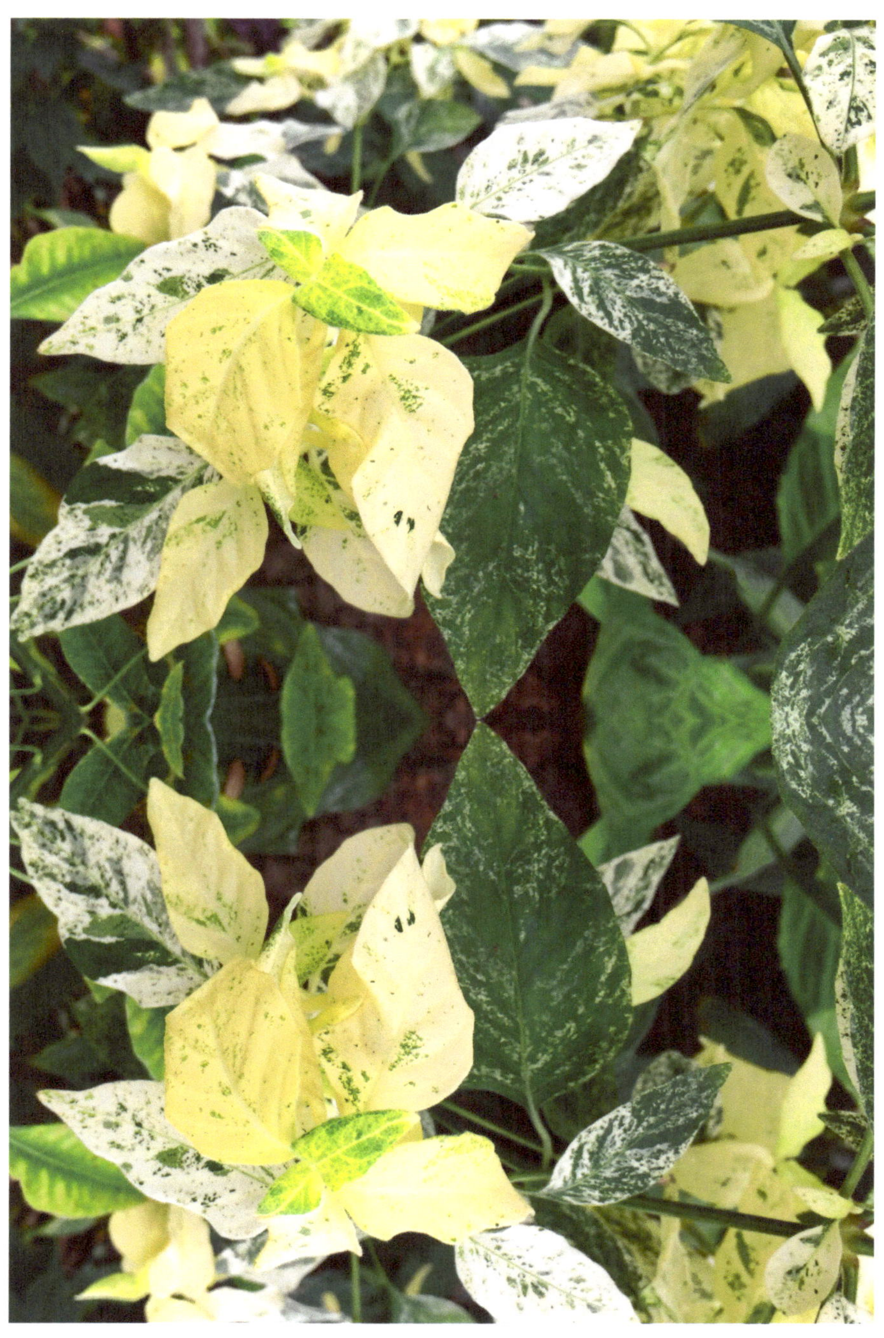

Zoom to Heaven

Zoom to Heaven
If only it could be

I'd call you right away
You've been gone for so long

Would I see a younger you?
Or at the age when you were called Home

Would you be muted?
Would you only hear me?

If I were to put my hand on the screen
Would you feel its warmth on your face?

And if you did the same
Would you feel my tears?

Zoom to Heaven
If only it could be

I'd call you right away
I've missed you for so long

April 4, 2021

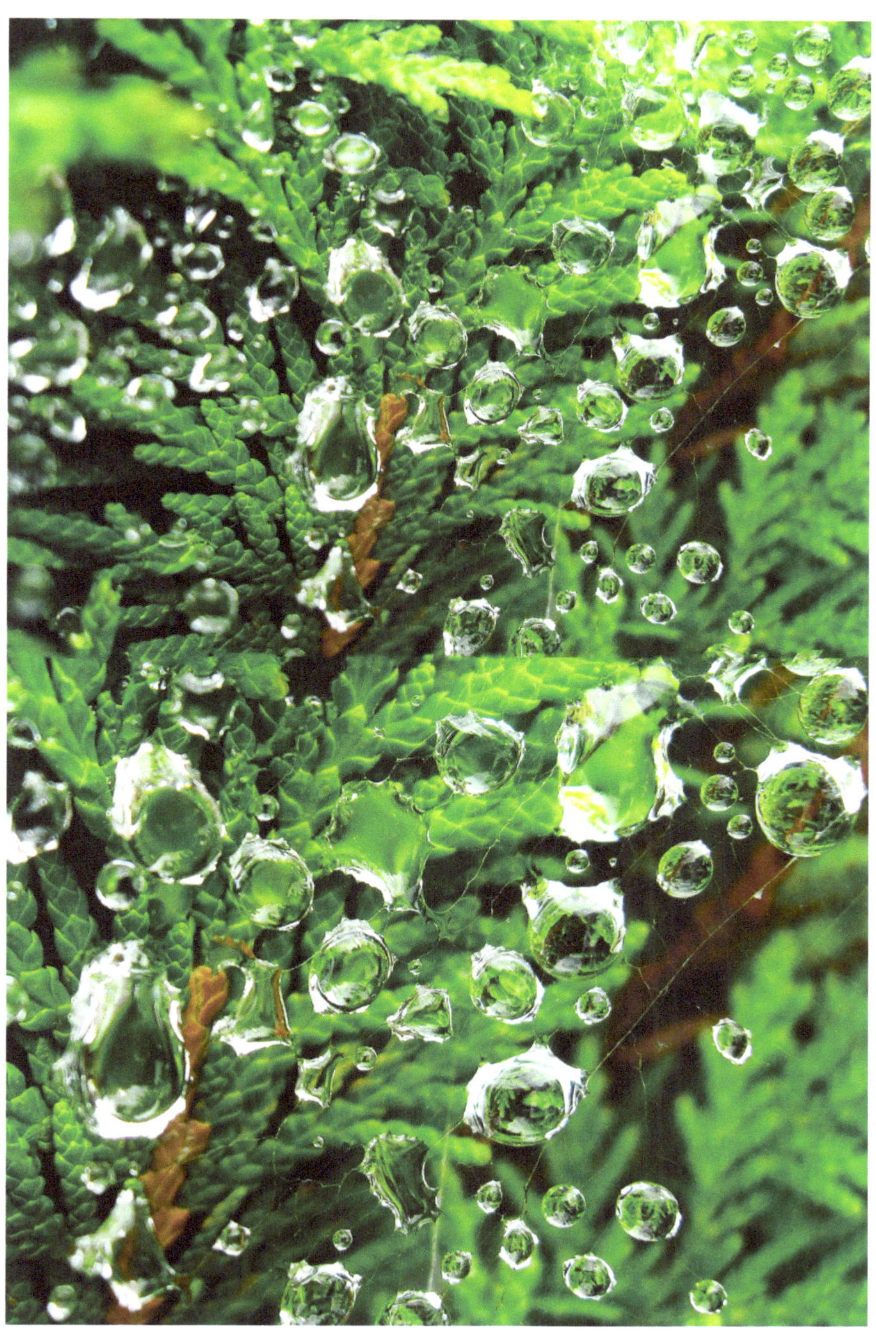

The most beautiful love poem

The most beautiful love poem
Has only three words

It was written for you
It was written for me

You would think
The words are: "I love you!"

But you would be wrong
Because the verse really means
"I love you that much!"

The most beautiful love poem
Has only three words
Spoken at the end of a long journey
Followed by
A fierce roaring scream

The most beautiful love poem
Will always be...

His words on the cross

The declaration of His perfect love

For you...

For me...

By our Saviour with pierced hands...

"It is finished!"

April 26, 2021

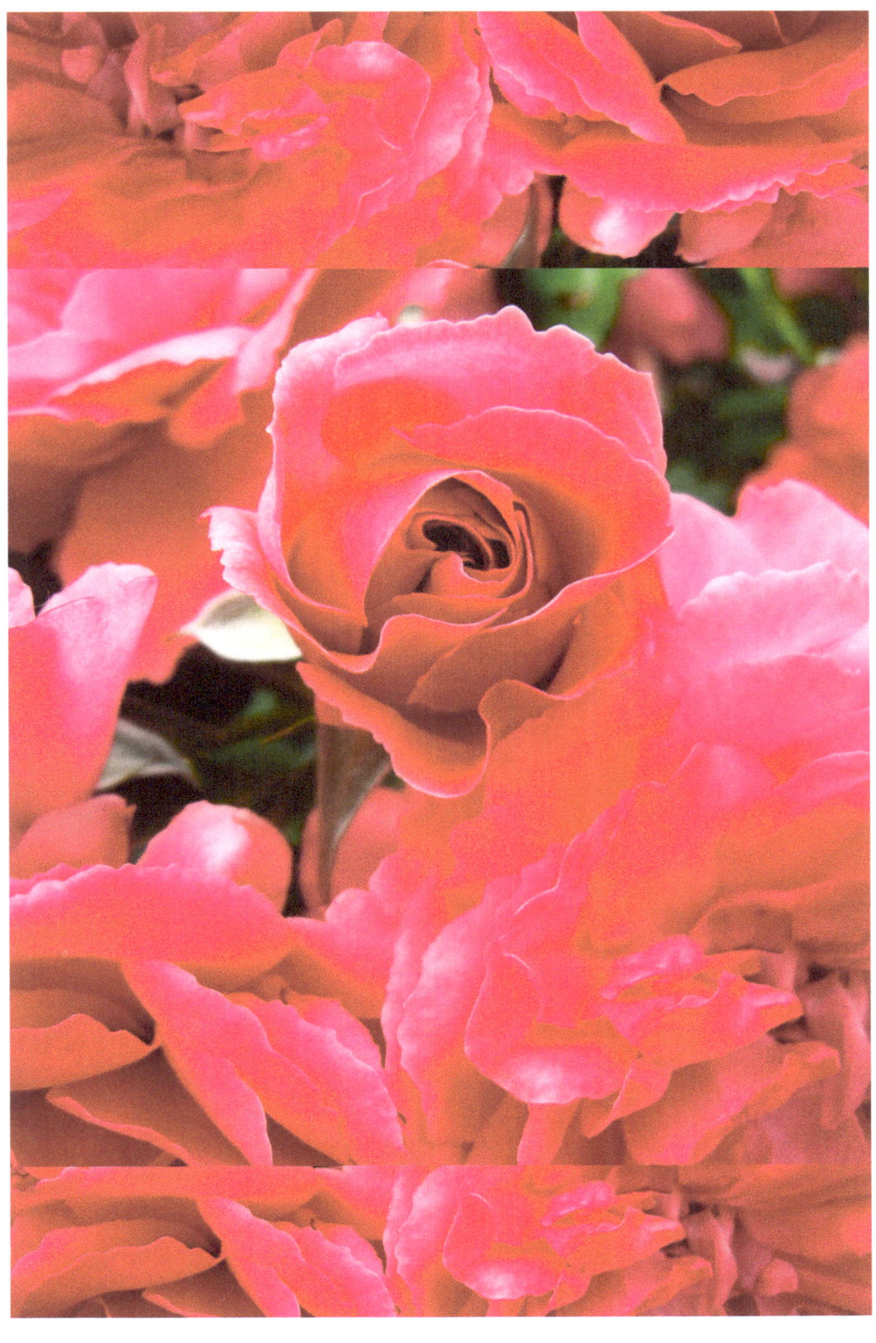

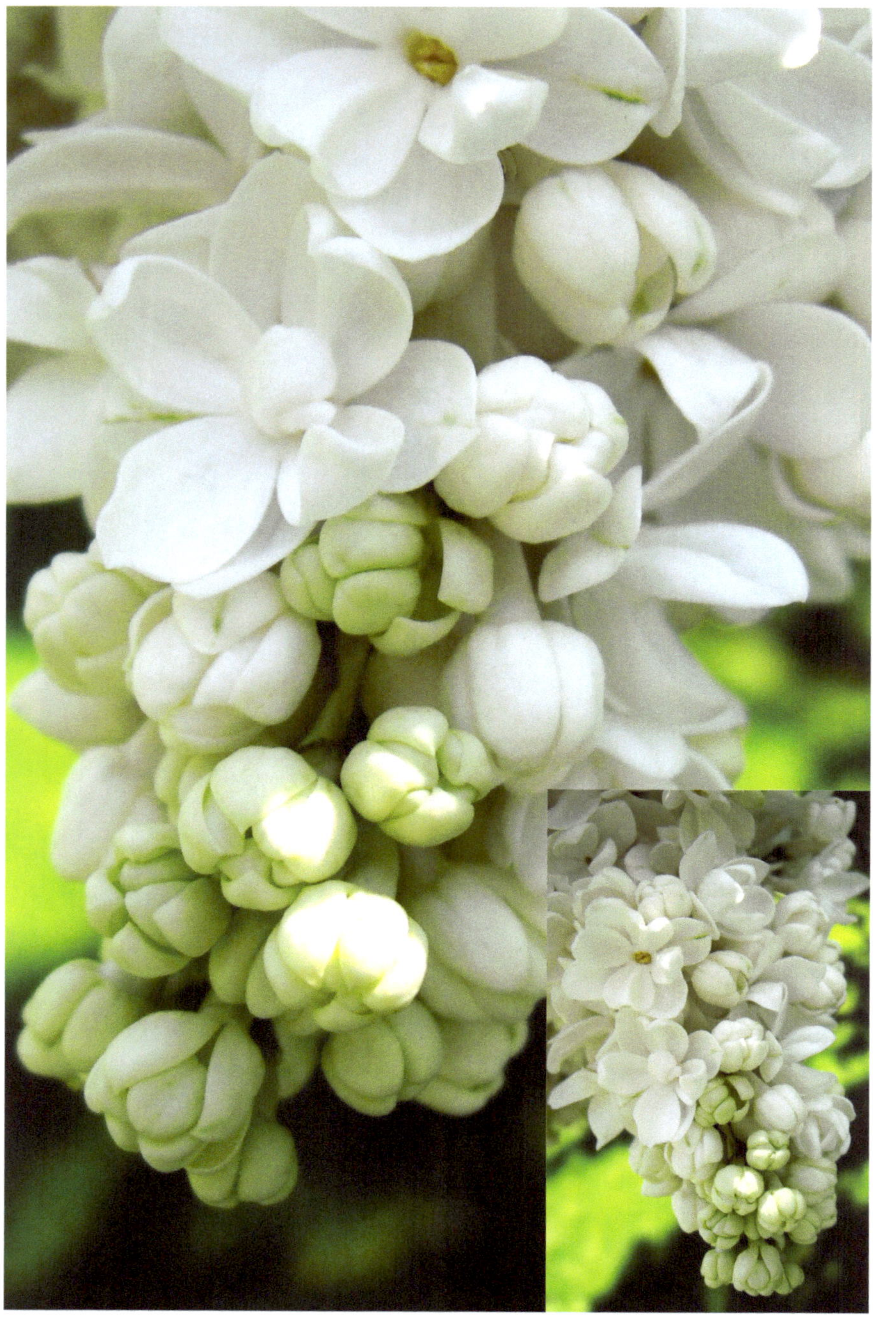

"Let there be light."

"Let there be light."

Colours...are combinations of three

For painters
It's red, yellow, and blue

And white, the absence of them

Surprisingly
It's different with lights

If you're on a stage
Then red, blue, and green
Are the coloured lights you'll need

Combine these three
And you'll see appear
In the center of them...
Bright white light

Is that what You did?
Only in reverse

"Let there be light."

Was it white?

God, when You created light
Was it white?

With all the colours in the world
The infinite combinations
Hidden inside

Did Your white light
Slowly separated itself in three?

Revealing red, blue, and green

And You started to paint

Inventing combinations
Spectacular colours
Gushing from Your light
Flowing everywhere

Embellishing Your creation
With gorgeous radiant colours

"Let there be light."

May 28, 2021

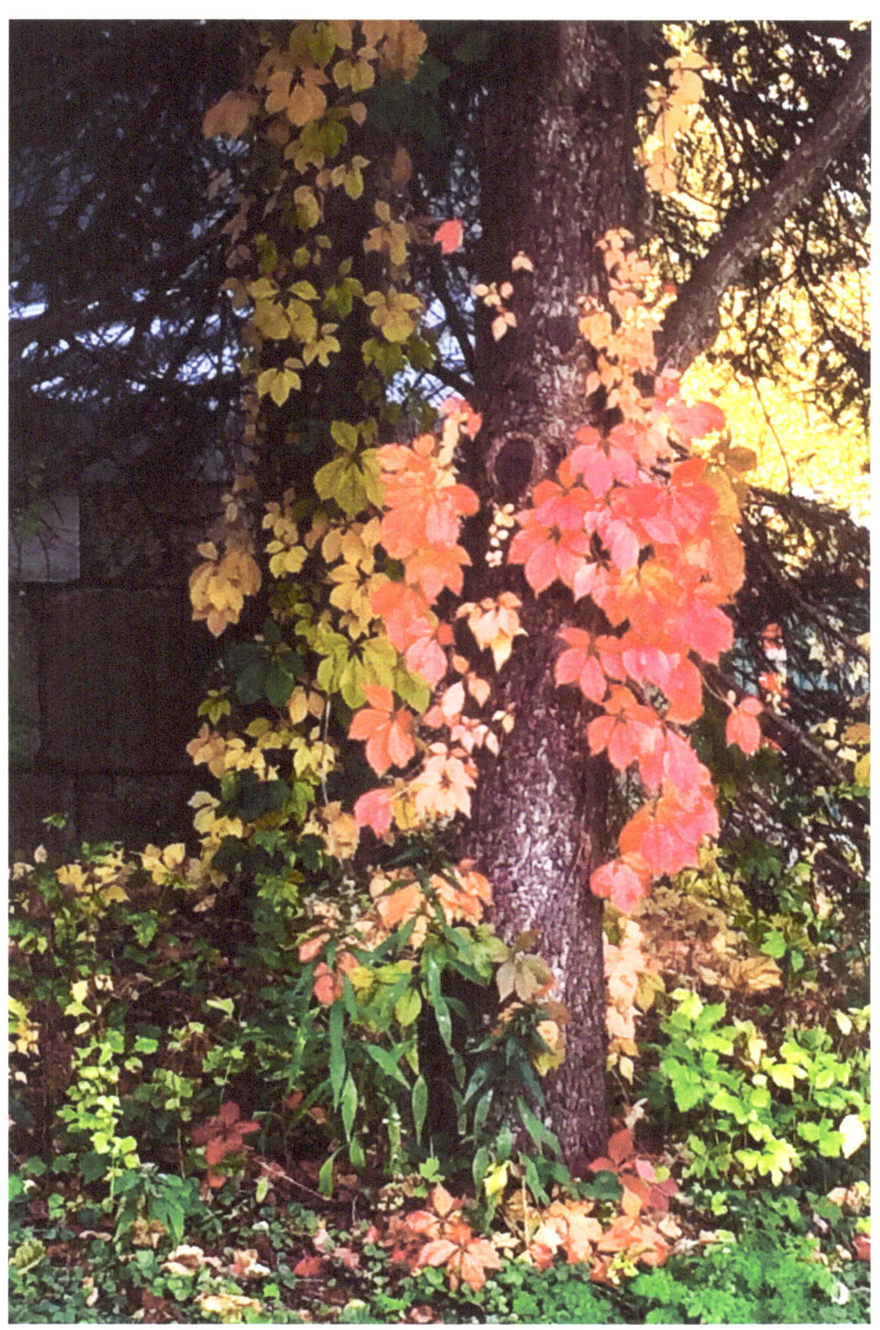